Feral Class

MARC GARRETT

<.:.Minor.:.>
.compositions.

Feral Class
Marc Garrett

ISBN 978-1-57027-439-8

Cover image by Marc Garett. Self-portrait: Blue Striped Angst. Oil on Board. 1986.
Cover design by Haduhi Szukis
Interior design by Casandra Johns

Released by Minor Compositions 2026
Colchester / New York / Port Watson

Minor Compositions is a series of interventions & provocations drawing from autonomous politics, avant-garde aesthetics, and the revolutions of everyday life.

Minor Compositions is an imprint of Autonomedia
www.minorcompositions.info | minorcompositions@gmail.com

Autonomedia
PO Box 568 Williamsburgh Station
Brooklyn, NY 11211

www.autonomedia.org
info@autonomedia.org

Table of Contents

Acknowledgements................5
About the Author.................9
Images & Illustrations.............11
Foreword 13
Introduction....................19
Fading Away...................23
A Memory in a Back Garden......27
The Discovery of Too Many
    Brothers and Sisters.........29
Marcus Brutus Patriarch Killer.....31
Propped Patriarch................33
My Mum the Dealer
    and My Life as a Shit..........35
A Drawer of Heroin...............37
Poor Bastard....................39
The Dead Crusaders............43
My Best Friend, Bobby...........45
Barry's Galleon Ship Disaster.....49
My Dad, Me, and the Genie........51
The Screamer...................55
Scars and Toy Rifle Pop Gun......59
Barry the Spider:
    Out of the Picture...........61
Black Magic, A Miscarriage,
    and Horror 63
Head Through the Window.......67
The Demonic Cat................69
Happy Family Stage Set..........71
The Wall of Death 73
Memories of Place and Drowning . 77
A Kick in the Chest..............79
Adopted for a Week.............81
A Suicide at the Picnic...........85
The Beast......................87
My Entrepreneurial Egg Venture .. 93
Battle at the Green..............95
Walking Metamorphosis.........99
Mr Crow 103
Vision On: My Betrayal..........105
A Wank, the Eleven-plus,
    and a Circumcision.........107

Golf and Class War..............111
The Death of Uncle Don..........115
The Great Escape................119
Gobbing on the Bobby...........123
She's a Witch!..................125
Revisiting the Vicarage...........127
How My Art Teacher
    Inspired Me................129
Geeky School Comrades
    and a Bar Mitzvah...........131
A Slump at the
    End of the Garden..........133
How a Library Saved My Life......135
When Mum Asked Me to Rent Porn
    from the Local Video Shop....137
Adventure in a Reliant Robin......141
The Valentines Card 143
Saturday Workers at Paul's
    Discount Clothing Store......145
Jumping in Front of a Bus.......149
My First and Last Boyfriend.......153
Blue Nick......................157
My Brother and Hitler............159
Nigel and Fire..................163
Fighting Nazis on a Train.........167
Shoplifting Memories............171
Silent Command 177
Punk Hangouts and Havens
    in Essex...................181
Natalie........................187
Simon and Perry................191
York Road Market Jobs..........195
Early 1980s Anarchism
    in Southend................197
Cha, Cha, Cha, Changes 201
Sympathy for the Runt..........205
The Useless Sea................209
Masters of the Universe..........211
The Shame of Leaving
    and Returning..............213
A New Life.....................215

Acknowledgements

THE FIRST PERSON I SHOULD THANK IS MY MOTHER, Maria. She died about five years ago but strongly influenced me; this book significantly features her. I want to thank my brother Nigel. Twelve years ago, when cycling home on his way back from building work, he was killed by a youngster in a speeding car. It was a tragic time for all the family. Nigel is also highly featured in this writing. I miss Mum and him very much. Then there is Samantha and Zoe, my younger twin sisters, who have been inspirations and amazing siblings through the years. I've always valued their endless sense of humour, no matter how tough things have been for them, the rest of the family, and close friends.

The book focuses on my life up to 1987. But I still should say a big thanks to Ruth, my wife and life collaborator since 1996. It hasn't been easy not to slip her into the book more, especially when her critical thoughts and suggestions regarding the ideas, processes, and discussions around it all have been so precious. Since we met, life has been an adventure that has involved constant, intense dialogue, critical thinking, and profound, imaginative challenges. She has a soul, and I am so glad we met. It has taken us years of mental agility to deal with each other's cultural differences. No one left on the planet knows me as much as she does. Ruth has bravely lived through my constant angst when dealing with class division in everyday life and snobbery in the arts and other creative sectors.

Punk, post-punk, and grassroots political folk music have also helped me understand the imaginative aspects of being part of the working and feral classes. For instance, Graham Burnett's comprehensive book Southend on Zine connects directly to my history as a teenager and in my early twenties in Southend-On-Sea.

Regarding academic and activist publications, there's the five-hundred-page monster of a book by Jonathan Rose, *The Intellectual Life of the British Working Classes*, published originally in 2002 and reprinted in 2021. It is a landmark book providing an intellectual history of the British working classes from the preindustrial era to the 20th century. Another book that introduced emancipation alongside historical allies is Edward Palmer Thompson's influential book *The Making of the English Working Class* (1963). He challenged the prevailing opinion that the working class benefited from industrialisation (they demonstrably did not) and long-standing dismissals of radical figures and movements, such as the Luddites. In particular, he points out that the working class was far from mindlessly anti-technology or just trade unionists but capable of considerable feats of clandestine organisation and political-economic awareness.

And how can I forget Stewart Home, an English artist, filmmaker, writer, pamphleteer, art historian, and political activist? His work has reflected the politics of the radical left, punk culture, the occult, and the history and influence of the Situationists and other radical left-wing 20th-century anti-art avant-garde movements. Another individual and a good friend whom I consider to be a compassionate comrade who managed to bring about Marxism beyond academic elites is Richard Barbrook. He gave me faith that not all Marxists are middle-class snobs hiding in academic silos, ignoring the lower classes via convenient defaults.

Lisa McKenzie, whom I have gotten to know over the last few years, has been an unstoppable force fighting for the working classes. I have learned so much from her writings and genuine conversations on social media sites. Mckenzie's unusual and innovative approach weaves the academic world and working-class issues together as part of a quest for "real" emancipation; there is no lip service here. What makes her unique is that she's from a working-class background, which gives her credibility with the communities she works with. And she has always stayed true to her roots. Two of her publications worth reading are *Getting By: Estates, Class and Culture in Austerity Britain* and *Lockdown Diaries of the Working Class*.

Another publication I am grateful for is *Estates: An Intimate History* by Linsey Hanley, born and raised on the largest council estate in Europe, in London's East End, revisiting those days with a memoir and social history about those in Britain left behind. Both McKenzie and Hanley have been allies via their informative and grounded writings, offering insights and hope that I can also give recognition to my history and others while presenting critical, personal narratives where struggle may be difficult, but owning and sharing our own life stories can break down barriers in society. Like me, they both come from council estates and offer essential histories and perspectives on what it's like.

Cassie Thornton and her invaluable hands-on grassroots feral work, such as *The Hologram: Feminist, Peer-to-Peer Health for a Post-Pandemic Future*, has brought a network of grassroots care for all outside of establishment structures. Her feral entrepreneurship comes from a place which understands life on the ground, beyond the trappings of institutional hierarchies. Silvia Federici's book *Caliban and the Witch* is a brilliant historical study of the transition to capitalism from the Middle Ages, moving from the peasant revolts of the late to the witch-hunts and how the established elites were attacking the grassroots changes from serfdom to self-sufficient working classes. Crucially, Federici linked class struggle with the witch-hunts. Her text also resonates with me because my Mum was called a witch by various people, and we were unknowingly part of an underclass, often even unable to reach higher up the social ladder to be working class.

I would also like to thank Dani Admiss, Julie Freeman, Ann Light, Stacco Tronconso, and Jonas Frankki. All were essential at the beginning and during the writing process, offering their time, consideration, conversations, and support, which has been invaluable.

About the Author

MARC GARRETT GREW UP ON A COUNCIL ESTATE in Southend-On-Sea, Essex and left school in 1979. After working various jobs while attending college, he moved to a farm twelve miles outside Bristol and then to the city in 1987. From then on, Marc had an artist studio, made art in the streets, and co-ran the pirate radio station EMI (Electro Magnetic Interference). This was when he began taking writing more seriously and broadcasting working-class culture on pirate radio. He briefly moved to Birmingham in 1991 and ran public artists talks at the Icon Gallery. Then, he moved to London in early 1993. Between 1992–95, he worked as a co-sysop on several anarchist bulletin boards, including Cybercafe, an art and hacktivism community, while making street art, painting and digital art.

He was involved in a number of artist studio builds, first at Art in Perpetuity Trust, founded in 1995 by a group of artists in an old warehouse on Deptford Creek, London. After realising he couldn't afford the studio rent, Marc had to leave and, in 1995, joined a Bow Arts Trust where he was part of the team to establish The Nunnery Gallery.

In 1996, Marc and artist Ruth Catlow co-founded the organisation Furtherfield in response to Brit-Art and the Saatchi's dominance of art via marketisation, drowning out lesser-known artists. Collaborating with artists, techies, and activists exploring similar critiques worldwide, they built alternative art contexts and grassroots infrastructures on and offline. Experimenting with analogue and digital tools and networks to build bridges, demolish top-down hierarchies, and set the conditions for societal emancipation. Furtherfield is still going strong today.

Marc has widely published critical and cultural essays, articles, interviews, and books about art, technology, and social change. In 2017, he co-edited *Artists Re: Thinking the Blockchain* and, in 2022, published *Frankenstein Reanimated: Creation & Technology in the 21st Century*. After eight years of study, Marc finished a PhD at Birkbeck University, London, in 2021, during COVID-19. Using the autoethnographic research conducted for his PhD, he is now writing a book, *Furtherfield: 30 Years of Art, Technology, and Eco-Social Change of the Arts Collective Furtherfield*, reflecting on the communities established around two physical galleries and a community lab, the Furtherfield.

Since 2012, Furtherfield has run two venues in Finsbury Park, London. Marc has curated over 60 contemporary exhibitions and projects exploring art, technology, and eco-social change, as well as exhibitions and projects nationally and internationally. His other personal output explores contemporary society in a post-digital context and examines aspects of working-class culture as part of an intersectional enquiry.

In 2022, during COVID-19, he was diagnosed with cancer just after moving to Felixstowe, Suffolk. Since his gradual recovery, he has focused on ideas and questions that acknowledge and engage working-class and feral-class contexts as a springboard for more extensive dialogues on creating conditions for social change across art, technology, and ecology.

Images & Illustrations

23   Propped Patriarch. Pen on paper. 23 x 17 cm. From Sketchbook, 1986. Marc Garrett.

39   Sketch for Paranoia. Self-portrait, 1986.

43   Hanging on. Printed ink on paper, pastels and chalk. 1984.

51   The Genie. Drawing on A4. 2024.

67   Broken Again, Please Rebuild Me. Watercolour, Collage and drawing. A4. From Sketchbook, 1994.

71   Happy Family Stage Set. Ink drawing on card. 23 x 17 cm. From Sketchbook, 1987.

87   Fish Out of Water. 1986.

93   Egg Head. Crayon and pen on paper. 23 x 17 cm. From Sketchbook, 1986.

99   Walking Metamorphosis. Pen on paper. 23 x 17 cm. From Sketchbook, 1986.

173 Hitchy Samuels: The World's First Disposable Comedian. 1986.

192 David Wales and Perry. Photo supplied by David Wales.

198 Graham Burnett showing his punk zine, New Crimes, published 1981 on Southend on Zine minimovie by Aaron Shrimpton.

199 Autumn Poison – Live at The Railway Hotel, Southend-on-Sea, Essex – Saturday 7 May, 1983.

Foreword

"Every day, people are brilliant, and I don't need a PhD for that. The PhD was something I needed to prove to myself, and it contributed to me getting cancer; [it was] a passport to be feral in places that would normally not listen to you."

– Phone conversation with Marc on 2 August, 2024

THE FERAL CLASS IS WRITTEN BY AND ABOUT a member of an unidentifiable group of people who are simply too upset to assimilate and smile while standing on a planet we've turned into a predatory, combat economy. The unruly combination of factors that allow you to hold this book today demonstrates the work of Marc and the feral class. To be specific, this book's existence is a beautiful contradiction: an untamed, nonlinear, and emotional allegory of a person who took close notes on his own spiritual and embodied disobedience in the face of all forms of authority and privilege, especially concerning the violence of institutions, is published and distributed by a renowned academic press. It can appear as if the academy and its sister institutions, prisons, and pensions, professionalise and discipline all that is untameable and wild. What if a disorganised class of people were here to ruin that story?

Marc is one of the first people I ever met who could use an invitation to an esteemed institution built on a legacy of wealth, power, and exploitation to make a sincere offering that says and means, *eat the rich, you cunts,* very politely and with elegance. The feral class is an unsynchronised group of people who are not afraid to point out that the water is contaminated if it is obvious that someone has pissed in it. This unlinked network of dissidents cannot participate in a reality built on violent contradictions without pointing them out or disrupting them, though they (or, shall I say, we) are not necessarily strategic. In a way, to be strategic would be to play into the rules of the economy, rules that say everything has to be rational, and rationality has to do with a profitable bottom line, which makes no sense when we are on a burning planet. Being strategic might mean that we have a choice.

As Marc will explain, the feral class is not the working class, and membership in this class has nothing to do with one's ability to work to make money or to make sense. As he describes, the feral class might capture people dumped by the working class because we are too weird or disobedient. However, the feral class does do very important (unwaged) work – we use our emotional and bodily reactions to the discomfort of normativity to disturb, dismantle, or destroy structures that force us all to be workers (workers who smile through the pain we endure when we ignore the exploitation and colonial wars our capitalist lives are built upon). Our work in the feral class is to make a mess that exposes our individual and collective discomfort, even if that makes us slightly unemployable. But our work is not something assigned to us that we choose or that we can quit.

As the world gets hotter and the air conditioning bill goes up, many people with managerial class salaries or investments keep drinking better coffee, doing more rigorous exercise, and using faster computers. Meanwhile, those same people report anxiety, depression, and brain fog. Some of the benefits of the job are no longer satisfying. What if more and more of these contracted but never fully employed humans, often locked into academic jobs that afford these unsatisfying and incomplete distractions from global suffering, working for controlling but decently paying repressive institutions, may unconsciously desire an escape that they cannot imagine alone? What if the possibility of making a mess becomes more needed and valuable than ever? This is where people like me and Marc have and do come in – to moderate a panel, write an article, produce an exhibition or be an artist in residence. As uncategorisable people who can speak wisely without faith in the dying value system of the academic or other institution, we have both been professionally involved with exposing the contradictions that everyday people are contracted to work within and smile about. We do neither reform nor revolution; it is a kamikaze mission to break what needs to be broken. This is how I pay rent.

While I think the feral class is hugely "smart," I don't think our prowess is primarily intellectual or rational. The messy breaking and breaking down, which I see as a primary part of the work of the feral class, is rooted in an unfiltered bodily response to pain produced by systems of oppression. This isn't necessarily conscious. Animals may be seen as feral when they escape captivity. There isn't a possibility of leaving captivity as a human in capitalism. Maybe that's why feralness is presumed to be brutal, raw, unkind or unwanted when applied to humans living in capitalism – better to rule it out than to want what we can't have (and something unmarketable, ew!)? In a world defined by economic survival, feralness is unstrategic. Economic survival mainly involves ignoring one's body. For the feral class, maybe that doesn't work. *Does it work for anyone?*

When Marc was a young, upcoming artist, his body repeatedly gave him no choice but to be an anti-capitalist artist. In more than one scenario, Marc got sick when witnessing unchecked class privilege as well as the absurdity of the art market. When he first went to NYC in 1991, a smug curator invited him to Christie's or Sotheby's auction house (it doesn't matter which one; they are all the same in this context). Seeing his art heroes' work was valued at thousands of pounds, he "turned green, ran out, and threw up on the steps outside the building, and couldn't go back in." He told me he felt too ill, ill in a way that continues to affect him when he witnesses the worst, most extractive and ironic parts of the way in which culture cuddles up to toxic industries through getting involved with stuff like crypto, AI, and the elite art market.

In this collection, Marc shares many stories that involve him as a younger person struggling to contain his disgust for unfairness. These stories become weightier when we feel them within the context of Marc's professional life, including decades of vital contributions to cutting-edge critical working-class art and culture. I know Marc as a prominent and successful artist, co-founder and organiser of Furtherfield Gallery in London, a curator, writer, editor, DJ, academic and public speaker. His work as a critical utopian looks at technology, psychology, art, magic, film, pop culture, and class. This list of identities or interests does not do him justice, though. When Marc appears in institutionalised academic or art spaces, things change because, as in all of the stories told in this book, he doesn't shut out his aversion to unfairness or his high expectations for what we can achieve if we work together. His presence is unprecedented within institutional spaces, *including publishing*; he does an essential service of speaking up with honesty against the tacit wishes of institutions. Marc's difficult work to stay present in spaces that challenge him and that he challenges gives gravity to the vulnerable and outrageous stories he shares here. Because these stories of feralness and Marc's disgust with normativity are the foundation of his professional life.

The first time I heard Marc mention *Feral Class*, I was sitting on the floor drinking builders' tea at the coffee table in his and Ruth's new living room in Felixstowe. We were getting ready to watch music videos curated by Marc. I had just come to visit after I had finished a new performance, where I hired an actor/butoh performer to attend a conference about the future of critique after the Internet at one of the wealthiest cultural institutions in Germany. Furu, a Japanese man, attended one day of the conference on my behalf. At every session, he could be found crying, violently and sincerely, about the absurdity and disappointment of the costly and useless conference, populated chiefly by white cis men, held during what already felt like an environmental and social apocalypse. The curator of the conference and the Kunsthalle had commissioned me to make this performance called *THE VERY LAST CONFERENCE* as if he was willing to help me destroy his work. Afterwards, the curator presented me with a news article from Die Zeit about the conference that described Furu's performance as a request for more kindness in critique. When I asked the curator why he thought the well-known art journalist so fully misunderstood the project, I stopped hearing from him.

This performance followed a long series of work I have been doing since 2011, in a similar spirit to puking outside the art auction house, which I call *public breakdowns*. In this work, I hire actors to respond to something specific within an institution or event that seems customary because we are used to unseeing it, which is absurd or violent. The performers trained with me to throw tantrums or to cry, to create a space where time stopped, articulating a difficult feeling that would otherwise not be allowed into institutional space. This work began in 2011 when I hired an actor to play an art student for over a year at my costly private US art school. There she revealed the hysteria she experienced about the hundreds of thousands of dollars of debt she was incurring for a future of work that promised nothing. I have trained young men in the Czech Republic to have breakdowns about their relationship to gender and ableism within banks, bookstores, and universities. I have produced moments within massive business school lecture halls at Ivy League Universities where actors playing students become unhinged as they question some of the basic assumptions of macroeconomics, including scarcity, competition, and that we are an economic species. Most recently, I brought a feral class elderly person from the future to speak frankly at a tech conference, removing all the hype and sexiness from the space. Grandma couldn't stand the contradiction of drinking coffee, worshipping expensive digital art, and discussing how the world is burning. In each of these cases, I was brought in by a curator or administrator who knew what I was doing. In most cases, they were also disappointed. I made a mess, and it wasn't pretty.

After each of these projects, I usually have a (little) breakdown. It takes a lot out of me. It is difficult and tiring to encounter harsh capitalist reality (or, here, the institution) and be disappointed; to unconsciously seek transformation, and not know how to do it. It doesn't feel like a plan or a choice. It is a weird compulsion, and it can lead to many different behaviours. Maybe the weirdest one is to move deeper into the spaces that make us feel so bad, the way I and Marc have. When speaking to Marc in the months since his recovery from cancer, I see him entering institutional spaces less and less. I see him doing a lot of slow and gradual work to undo some of the habits that got him sick in the first place. He is making decisions about where to put his energy and when. I don't think that was always true for him based on the opening quote, where Marc describes how his PhD was something he needed to prove to himself – a passport to go be feral where he wasn't otherwise allowed – and how the PhD contributed to his cancer.

What if the feral class shows us that our bodies are connected to a planet set ablaze by careless and violent human behaviour? To constantly feel like puking is not abnormal, given the circumstances, but most of us have had to shut that out. But if we stop collaborating with the body's signals and needs, we get even sicker. I relate to this. I learned from writing this essay that we all may belong to the feral class, but we may not know how to let ourselves know it or be it. This book is a passport to be a member of an unrecognisable, disorganised class here to ruin some of our most boring stories, and it won't make you sick.

Cassie Thornton
Berlin, November 2024

Introduction

THIS BOOK IS AN ACCOUNT OF A WILD JOURNEY. As a white male who grew up in poverty on a rough 1970s council estate in Southend-on-Sea, Essex, I have experienced class oppression all my life. This book revisits my earlier life up to 1987 and has been a powerful force and grounding influence on my life while simultaneously being a constant mystery to me. Unearthing our history has been especially rewarding because it has helped me understand my Mum's life, psychology, and social context. My mother has been a powerful force and a grounding influence on my life while simultaneously being a constant mystery. This book would not exist without the memory of her, her ghost, or traces of her, reminding me about certain past moments, situations, and their effects on me then and now. It is through her that I have learned about women. Thankfully, her influence has opened my heart and mind to how the patriarchy has ruled women and men through the centuries.

Certain films, such as *A Taste of Honey* resonated with me from a young age. Made in 1961 and written by Shelagh Delaney, three years before I was born, this kitchen sink drama, or a social realist film, it starred Rita Tushingham. I remember watching it with my Mum – it affected her; the story must have somehow reflected what she had been going through. Tushingham play a young girl who becomes pregnant after a short liaison with a black sailor who then departs. She befriends a gentle, kind-hearted gay man and sets up a home with him. Growing up, this introduced me to appreciate those who were not the same as me while learning about other people from working-class communities not the same as mine. The same goes for *Kes*, by Ken Loach, in 1969, a portrait of working-class Northern England. It's the story of a fifteen-year-old miner's son who finds solace and spiritual freedom in his deep bond with a wild kestrel, offering him an escape from his bleak life. Loach's moving coming-of-age drama remains the most beloved and influential film of the now-legendary director. *A Taste of Honey* and *Kes* were profoundly influential films for me. But there were also others, such as *Cathy Come Home* (1966), an early television feature by Loach. Other films include *Scum* and *Quadrophenia*, both released in 1979, which I discuss further in the book.

One example of a convenient default is when I applied for a PhD about ten years ago. An external examiner commented negatively about me, discussing aspects of my class and background. She said that I was glamorising my history as if I was in Shane Meadows' cult film *This Is England* (2006) and its three sequels (2010–2015). The critique floored me, and I felt I was being treated as a self-parody. It was the early days of the PhD, and a proposition for the study to be an autoethnography was gradually emerging as my methodology. What was interesting is that I had never watched any of Meadows' films, because they felt to me like poverty porn, just like the TV series, *Shameless*. However, I was accepted onto the PhD course because those more directly involved in lecturing me knew it was real and that denying my voice was wrong.

Yet, what I experienced from that individual criticizing my approach towards discussing my class background in the PhD was not unusual, especially when it came to middle-class people. Many a time, people have either labelled me as having a chip on my shoulder that I am performing as working-class as if I was meant to be something else or aspiring to get rid of my roots. My history is not a disposable object that can be deemed irrelevant. In fact, through the years, it has become even a stronger focus while adapting to everyday culture. If I ever forget other people's grounded histories, contexts, or circumstances, maybe that'll be the time to forget mine.

There is a lot relating to how myself, my family, and others have been shaped and how society has also transmuted us through its systems of dominance. This writing is a nod towards those who have struggled through generations of poverty and oppression. These are my people: we share a deep, structural and personal pain, not necessarily accompanied by an understanding that could bring us together. In reality, the media and everyday politics divide many of us. But strong, earthy, messy links bind the feral class and the working class together through because we are attacked by the same enemies and face similar struggles, even if we disagree about who these enemies are. Even if I disagree with right-wing, working-class and feral-class cultures, I know where they are coming from as people who have been forgotten and left behind. I disagree with their actions but understand why they exist. I'd be the same if I had not found a way out. I see myself as lucky. But it's not about being lucky, moving up a social ladder and leaving others behind. It's about challenging the myth of meritocracy and changing the systems that create social division.

The chapters are chronological. However, the timeline is just one way of approaching the material. Another way I envisaged was for readers to jump into the book at any point. The chapters are short, and each has strengths that define its elements, narratives, and stories. Finally, here are a few words about the images included in the book: some are personal family photographs; others are under the Creative Commons Attribution 2.0 Generic license. Then, there are my own images, including early drawings and paintings. Many of the pictures included were created at the time of the experience written about. Others were produced a bit later and are personal reflections on the memories discussed. Much of this material is from sketchbooks containing my thoughts, observations, and feelings in the form of texts and images.

WHY FERAL CLASS?

I use the term working class as peer recognition and cultural alliance with others who view themselves as working class. But I'm sure the label is not necessarily an adequate representation for many. The term working class has always been broad for me, relating to varied social sections, conditions, and theories of political organisation. The difference between the feral and working class is that the working class has a history of organised collective struggle around labour, building solidarity, shared values, and cultural identity. Hundreds of years of critical thought and actions have forged paths for working-class empowerment. The working class is a subset of waged workers or salary-based contracts whose exact membership varies from definition to definition. Members of the working class rely primarily upon earnings from wage labour. Socialists define the working class as those with nothing to sell but their labour – the proletariat.

Feral class is different, but there is some cross over. It's less structured and has no systems of official wages nor taxes. The feral class has strong links with the underclass and is made up of people who are very poor and have very little power or chance to improve their lives, the lowest of all social classes. So, I'm working class, but also feral class. I am a dysfunctional vagabond who tries to negotiate one's existence in a world of chaos and top-down dominance, where fate and systems designed against the working class and the feral class combined operate as heartless mechanisms to flip us around without care or consideration. I experienced my early life through a combination of events announcing themselves as unstoppable interruptions. My path was not going to be steady and straightforward; it was going to be precarious, fearful, violent, confusing, and filled with anxiety.

Barry, my (blood) father, was knowledgeable and university-educated but also a drug dealer working undercover for Scotland Yard as an informer. Life with him constantly distracted one's intimate space and personal growth. Mum was orphaned at three and came from a large East End working-class family. Much of the family's history relates to working on East India Docks in Blackwall, East London, north-east of the Isle of Dogs. When my Mum moved to Southend-On-Sea in the late 1960s, times were hard because there was no reliable work structure. Existence constantly relied on clandestine ways of finding money. For example, I sometimes wonder whether my Mum was a sex worker before I was ten. I have no evidence of this, only strange feelings and suspicions.

I have never been convicted of a crime, but my mother and Barry have, and my brother spent time in Borstal. Some of my mum's brothers were East End gangsters and thieves, always getting into trouble. For some reason, even though I had my fair of scrapes, I have tended not to want to get involved with criminal activity. My brother used to deal drugs at my mum's house, and she must have known, but I'm not sure. I've always had an affinity with outsiders, whether Roma, new-age travellers, punks, activists, artists, or people without homes. It includes feeling genuine respect and allegiance with women, the Irish, people of colour, queer and transgender people, and others who have and continue to struggle to exist in a tediously conservative, elitist, neoliberal, and imperialist colonial society.

OK. I think you're ready. Welcome to the feral odyssey.

Fading Away

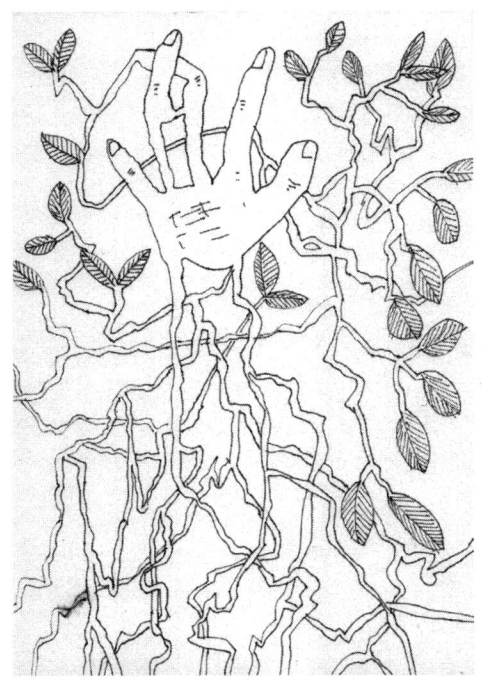

CANCER IS ONE OF THE MOST TRAUMATIC EXPERIENCES I've ever had, and I've had a few. I was diagnosed on the same day Russia invaded Ukraine, 24 February 2022, so the day was already feeling bleak. At about 10.30 am, Ruth and I were guided into a small room in the hospital, which was where they gave us the distressing news that I had cancer. At that time, I had a lump the size of a large lemon sticking out of my neck, so we knew something was up, although I was hoping it wasn't cancer. It was overwhelming. There were about eight to ten medical staff with different specialisations concerning neck cancer. Each of them talked me through what would happen to me, what they'd be bringing to the table, and which part of the treacherous journey they were involved in.

After my cancer treatment, which involved six weeks of intense chemotherapy and radiotherapy five days a week, life changed immediately, and I gradually, through the weeks of treatment, got worse. For example, I couldn't consume food orally, so they planted a tube into my stomach, feeding me liquid food and medicines. Walking was difficult. I could only walk a few feet before sitting down. My body just didn't have the energy. Various symptoms occurred because of the treatment, such as spitting out radiation phlegm non-stop, for months. I caught thrush in the throat twice. I was put into intensive care twice. Once it was for pneumonia, a collapsed lung, and low oxygen levels for ten days. The second time, a large abscess grew on the side of my neck, about half the size of a football, due to infections in the salivary glands. I was in hospital for three weeks.

On the first night of my first stay, I was put in critical care. It was a rough night and in the early morning, at about 3.30 am, I woke up and looked at what seemed like a fuzzy cloud shimmering before me. I imagined the cloud was someone trying to contact me from the dead. It felt like my mind was playing tricks on me. Once I had gone back to sleep, I dreamed that my dead brother and mother were calling for me. As I searched for them, my breathing became less frequent, and my heart rate slowed. But I couldn't find them. There was nothing, no one, only emptiness and silence. In the morning after the strange dream, the nurses said my heart rate had slowed down to a dangerous level, and I could have died. I did wonder where the staff were when my brush with death was taking place. Thankfully, I clawed my way back from the emptiness.

The image on the previous page was drawn on the same morning after I nearly died. The idea of me disappearing into nothingness did bring about some deep concerns. I remember as a young kid in bed one night, laying on my back with my eyes closed, trying to see inside my mind's eye, asking myself what it would be like if I was dead. What made it confusing was that a larger and more spacious feeling and vision of the universe appeared. The vastness felt cold and pointless. This lonely existential feeling made me cry; my insides felt empty, and I was terrified. The thing is, I wasn't crying just for myself. I was crying for everyone. From that point,

I have either noticed, presumed, or imagined another's deep emptiness. It doesn't always happen. Only if I allow a specific emotional energy to take over will this feeling be less frequent as time passes, not because it doesn't exist in me anymore. But I've realised this assumed profundity is a distraction from noticing the context of other things. Looking into the darkness is not necessarily the only way of engaging but part of the more nuanced complexity of life, death, and whatever else is happening.

Every few days, Ruth visited me in the hospital. I could hardly walk. She took me out of the ward in a wheelchair downstairs into a local garden, part of the hospital grounds. Around this period, I was at my weakest. The cancer treatment had taken its toll, and we thought I might not even last another week. The cancer ward was a suffocating environment, and experiencing many other people's various levels of cancer and their pain also hit me with an abject and raw existential feeling 24/7. I felt imprisoned, and looking out of the windows from inside the ward, re-emphasized how much I missed the world outside. It all felt so distant, potentially the past. Most of the time, I couldn't eat or drink anything besides water. Whenever I escaped to the small outdoor garden with Ruth, it was a sanctuary where we could sit in peace. Those moments were precious. I remember watching small birds flying around and listening to them chirping away; it felt magical.

I owe a debt to the NHS. They saved my life. What an amazing service it is. I am grateful that all UK citizens have the right to access free health services offered by doctors, nurses, midwives, and dentists without paying directly. I can't imagine what it's like in the US, which seems such a callous place to exist if you are poor.

Well, I'm back! I was told I am now in remission. Generally, this means the treatment has reduced or eliminated cancer from inside the body. This book is an opportunity to present a side of myself that has remained separate from my work in art, technology, and social change over thirty years. My mother had an amazing life, and at various times, I suggested she needed to write a book about it all. er story could help others take ownership and reclaim their societal contexts and histories. She spent most of her time on this planet struggling to exist and making sure her children survived. She only had the time to do it when she was in her 70s, but by then needed a damn good rest. So, I'm writing about segments of my life instead. Her spirit lives all through the writing, alongside mine and others included. It also feels like my last chance to share my roots and unpack how my past has shaped and guided me when being and working with others. This book is one of various things I must do before leaving this exhilarating and magnificent life. While writing this text, I realised what the image was saying. I'm still here, not gone. Not yet.

A Memory in a Back Garden

I'M NOT SURE WHO TOOK THE PHOTOGRAPH. It could have been me. I was quite young then, so perhaps not. My first dad, Barry, probably took it. It's a photo of my Mum standing in the back garden. She stands straight and proud with her arms at her side, eyes closed, and her head facing the sky. She's bathing under the sun. Maria was a sun worshipper.

Mum used to have very long black hair that reached below her backside. Also, she had very dark skin and received many racist comments even though she was white. One of her favourite musicians in the late 1960s was Buffy Sainte-Marie, an Indigenous Canadian-American (Piapot Cree Nation) singer-songwriter, musician, composer, visual artist, educator, pacifist, and social activist. Listening to Sainte-Marie's music takes me back to a mysterious time when my parents experimented with life. Sainte-Marie's music felt magical then, and it still does. My mother was fascinated by Native American Indians and their indigenous values in contrast to the white invaders in the US. The irony now is that Sainte-Marie has recently been accused of misrepresenting her Indigenous roots. I'm not sure my Mum would care that much if she was still alive. I still value her contribution to influencing generations against colonisation.

Maria was feral. She was a hopeful, independent, intelligent, working-class woman. This picture always reminds me of her free spirit and how indifferent she was to tedious, conservative expectations. I have always deeply valued her wild and energetic spirit. She was more than a mother; she was a comrade fighting against the world and the ignorance of male stupidity and violence. I have never idolised her, but I grew up with a woman struggling against systemic patriarchy. She knew this, not as someone who identified as feminist but as a working-class woman oppressed by a male-dominated society and the sexist men who abided by the top-down rules and exploited these conditions unquestioningly. And this spirit of battling against such terrible human woes is in my DNA, part of my psyche. Ever since childhood, I've been engaged in various struggles against small and large oppressions. Yet, this chronicle is more complex than what is right or wrong or a quest towards enlightenment or perfection. Just like the most interesting things concerning humans, it's about looking at the less discussed terrains in life.

The Discovery of Too Many Brothers and Sisters

ABOUT FOUR YEARS BEFORE MY MUM DIED, there was an unexpected knock on the door at my mum's house. She answered it and met her brother, Frank, for the first time. She must have been seventy-four years old at that point. The rest of the family was very excited, but my Mum said that it was all too late now and that it was a lot to deal with at the tail end of her years. Her attitude regarding my and Nigel's sister being taken away by social services when I was eight and never seen again was that if Donna wanted to meet Mum and the family, she would have been in touch.

Maria had been put into an orphanage between 18 months to three years of age. She then grew up as a young girl in various foster homes and convents. From what she told me, they were a very violent environment to grow up in. These experiences had a dramatic effect on her later life. Frank had informed her she had another eleven siblings. Until then, she had thought there was only her, her brother Peter, and sister Beatrice.

Ruth and I drove Mum to Twickenham to meet Frank and his wife, Brenda. It was a fascinating experience. Even though they had not met, they immediately got on very well. It was uncanny – it was like they were both children again. They had the same sense of humour and even looked like each other. After that day, they saw each other now and then until Maria died.

Frank gave me the above photo showing my grandad and his local amateur football team, White Hart Lane FC, in Tottenham, London in the 1940s. Frank marked two players, which he believed may be his and Mum's dad, on the right side of the picture. He also had a few other facts about our family's history going back to the 13th century. For example, many of my ancestors were clockmakers, signmakers, and tradespeople. Not just that, many of them were Quakers. If I was going to become religious, Quakerism has always felt like my type of thing. Most of the people I know who are Quakers are left-wing and care for others in society beyond themselves. However, I'm aware this may be a rose-tinted view. Another aspect I appreciate about Quakers is their practice of gathering for worship, where the service follows an unplanned order, is largely silent, and may include spontaneous vocal ministry from attendees. People can reflect on each other's circumstances as part of a collective process.

Before Frank turned up at her door, throughout all her life, Mum believed her birth mother was Spanish and her father was Italian. She was told this once she was in the orphanages, and grew up thinking it was true and a part of who she was until her early seventies. So, when she discovered she was not as "exotic" as presumed, she had to reassess her life and its meanings. Her supposed parents were rich. Her mum had died of sadness in her large home in Hampstead when she got the news that her Italian husband, who was a fascist, was killed while charging against the enemy on his horse. The story about her parents was very romantic and explained why she had darker skin than everyone. I grew up thinking like she did because that was what she told me. Mum preferred her pretend history instead of the new, real version. Don't get me wrong, she took it all in and accepted it, but I knew she was yearning for something less normal. Yet, my sisters and I have been very happy to discover these new snippets of ancestry. At least, it helps us all a bit more and gives us grounding.

Marcus Brutus Patriarch Killer

WHEN I WAS BORN, my Mum initially wanted to name me Marcus Brutus, which would have been interesting to carry around with me through school and while living on a council estate. I suspect my survival chances would have been worth studying. How many other children have been given names that set them off to be bullied or experience particular issues due to what others see as silly names? Elon Musk and Grimes named a daughter, Exa Dark Sideræl, whom they call "Y," and their son, X Æ A-Xii, who goes by "X." I'm surprised Musk did not name his son Darth Vader.

I was born on the 15th of March, the infamous Ides of March, in Billericay Hospital. Roman senators murdered Julius Caesar at a senate meeting on this day in 44 BC led by his friend, Marcus Junius Brutus. A nurse persuaded my Mum not to give me this name, so I was called Marc instead. My father, Barry, was not present at the hospital for my birth, and to this day, I've never known why. Yet, through the years, Mum regularly reminded me that Marcus Brutus was her preferred name for me, saying I was the killer of the patriarch, which always made me feel uncomfortable. I was unsure why my Mum favoured this name above the one in the end given to me. It took a long time, years later, for me to realise just how much it suits me. I have always had an instinctive urge to topple patriarchy wherever I found it. I grew up with two fathers who both mistreated my Mum and me. Noticing what men were and are like domestically has created a negative view of them. I have also fought various battles against dominating bullying men, whether in education, work, politics, the arts or academia, my entire life.

Propped Patriarch

MY TWO FATHERS did not express or share their love. When they were about, it was usually intense and traumatic, with no feeling for my brother and me, no comfort, joy or relaxation. One of the issues I've had with writers such as Marx is that he concentrated on class within the capitalist organisation of labour and how the male proletarian exists within its systemic, elite frameworks. He was way ahead of his time discussing the industrialisation of working-class communities under the regimes of top-down hierarchies, but was blind to how women have been perpetually suppressed even more by the controlling power of capitalism and its state-imposed hierarchies. Yet, just as much as the working classes needed a revolution against the dominating levers of capitalism, it has also always needed a revolution against the patriarchal defaults that have insidiously been implemented and accepted as normal in society. In a working-class culture, where women are treated as inferior to men, even in terms of basic humanity, the consequence of Marx's neglect to demonstrate a route for the emancipation of females is a massive tragedy.

My Mum the Dealer and My Life as a Shit

ABOUT A YEAR BEFORE MY MUM DIED in 2021 she mentioned something that resonated with me. It was connected to a segment of a story I wrote in the 1990s. Mum said she had now and then dealt drugs in a local park while wearing an extra-large coat. The coat had many pockets of different sizes that she had sewn into the fabric. The coat was used to sell all sorts of drugs to Barry's customers. Until my Mum told me, I had no idea she had done this. But I must have known before because, in my short story *My Life as A Shit*, I wrote about a character who did something similar.

However, *My Life as A Shit* featured a renegade male scientist who joined a small group of activist scientists. The protagonists no longer wanted to have their ideas and energies consumed by large, soulless, military-funded organisations extracting their knowledge for war and killing the planet. It was written at the beginning of the World Wide Web in 1994. These radical pioneers explored their agency as part of an expanding world, communicating and connecting beyond traditional top-down, centralised systems.

They invented a machine that transferred consciousness into other beings and objects. After experimenting with various items and their bodies, Darnley, the main character, decided to try something else and, for some reason, felt emotionally connected to all kinds of excrement. Below is an extract of our lead character pondering as he sits on a park bench:

> What type and variety of individuals pace around here? I do not know what kind of fetish or desire anyone has in this place, yet everyone has something which is either a secret or a practice hidden well away from the prying world. It always astounds me that billions of people are on this planet, and most possess a unique passion. I have a shoebox, and to continue the experiment, I have to find a fresh dog turd.

Darnley had intended to collect his own dog's shit while walking his dog in the park. He had intended to use the turd as a host to transmute his consciousness into. It has been his dream to fulfil since I was a teenager. But before he picked up his dog's poo and placed it in a shoebox, he was distracted by the sudden appearance of a tramp offering an alternative. The vagrant revealed an assortment of see-through plastic bags consisting of different sizes of dog shit from inside his coat. After haggling, Darnley makes a deal for one of the shits in the tramp's trench coat for his dog's. They swap, and our protagonist receives a top-quality, moist, Great Dane turd. Unfortunately, further into the story, we learn that his decision to swap created a journey so hazardous that he ended up as an exhibit at the National Museum, the first human being transmuted into a turd because he couldn't return to his original form.

It was an unsettling feeling that Darnley met a guy in a trench coat selling his shit. Mum said she didn't deal drugs on Barry's behalf for long and deliberately tried to keep it away from the home. When his extreme association with drugs, gangs, magic, violence, and hot-headed associates began to cause trauma to the whole family, she swiftly turned against it. It's hard to grasp what was going through their minds then. Life was a rollercoaster, and much of it was visceral; there was also a fantasy side. I'm unsure whether the drugs got to me, but I remember lying in bed a few times looking at the curtains, and they seemed to be alive and spinning around. For all I know, I could've been tripping on LSD or mushrooms, but I don't think so. Because there was so much to deal with, it made me experience the equivalent of being seasick.

A Drawer of Heroin

ONE OF THE TROUBLESOME ISSUES for any drug dealer who also happens to be a father is that your kids can get in the way. Barry's undercover job selling drugs to Southend's small drug groups on behalf of Scotland Yard was a job, I suppose. I don't think he had another one. The plainclothes detective Jack used to visit our house to meet Barry, and they spent hours discussing plans together. He would leave a large box for Barry whenever he left, and I never knew what was inside. However, one day, I was playing and found a bag of white powder in the dining table drawer. I was confused about why so many bags of flour were in the drawer. I ripped a bag open and threw its contents in the air, spinning around in a circle. Barry walked in and screamed out aloud. He pushed me away, and I cascaded onto the floor, feeling ill. That's the only time I came across drugs at home.

Whenever I tried to find out about earlier incidences from Mum, she was hesitant and mysterious. It wasn't until I was bout twelve, during Ken's patriarchal reign, that I realised what the white bags were. I would only get a clearer picture of my history through different people interacting with my mum. For example, it was only through listening to my Mum and Ken arguing about our time with Barry that certain memories would be backed up.

Poor Bastard

I DIDN'T KNOW I WAS POOR until John Lynham, my friend a couple of doors down the road, began wearing trendy clothes. At the time, bell bottoms were all the rage. We were playing football in the street with other friends who were wearing similar clothes. They said my clothing was old and ragged and that I wasn't wearing what they were wearing. I responded, "[Your] bell-bottom jeans look stupid, and why do we all have to look the same anyway?" Then, it hit me: my family was poorer than theirs. My friends were not well off but better off than our family. I realised my parents didn't have jobs, or at least not real ones where you pay taxes. Everyone else down the street seemed to be aware of this except me until that moment. It hurt me an awful lot knowing that others looked down on me. It hurt so much that I began to cry in front of the other kids.

The realisation that we were poor affected me emotionally at various levels. Yet, some of this existential angst stems from when my Mum briefly had some inheritance money when I was about three years old. I don't know who gave her the cash and how much there was, but it was around twenty thousand, which was a lot then. During the short period when there was money, Mum bought rich, stylish Italian clothes and shoes for herself and had handmade clothes ordered for me. Before writing this, I had hoped to present here a couple of images to view. But sadly, no. Irritatingly, my photos of me at that age are still stored with my sisters. They don't know where as yet.

I last saw pictures of myself in the clothes my Mum had made for me six years ago at the council house when she was still alive. The two photographs that stood out for me were one showing me wearing a grey leather Lederhosen outfit and another showing me in a suit and a cap. I looked adorable and unusual. When John and friends expressed how unfashionable my attire was and reminded me how poor I was, I yearned to exist in a world where we didn't have to struggle. I wanted to be lifted out of the everyday pain.

Around the same time, other external situations aligned, which were also unsettling with life-defining aspects. For instance, whenever I hear the word "bastard" being used in a derogatory tone, it takes me back to school when I was about seven years old when other kids would insult me, calling me a bastard. Barry and my Mum did not marry. I wasn't sure what all the fuss was about. Yet, I did feel that I was supposed to accept this term as a kind of handed-down stigma, defining me as the wrong sort of child. I already knew in my very being that something wasn't quite right with me.

In a way, it was a reassuring badge to wear. What a silly insult. It didn't bother me if some idiot got all hot under the collar because of another person's circumstance; they had no choice. To use it as an example of who is not a decent human being is deeply shallow. I knew this even then.

However, what was more disturbing than the tedious insults was how dangerous a particular tree was. On the way to school in the mornings, I would run out of the ground-floor flat too fast, excited to start the day, then run straight into a tree. The thump of my head against the solid bark was hard, and my Mum had to pick me up off the floor several times. I soon learned not to run out of the flat, enacting the strange ritual of self-harm, and walked out instead, giving myself time to dodge the wooden obstacle.

Other things were going on around this time, and I began to create barriers between myself and the world I was interacting with. One example is when I pretended that I couldn't see the writing on the blackboard in class. I would blur my eyes to the point where they'd ache. The teacher suggested I have my eyes tested at the local clinic, which I did. Mum took me there, and I continued with the pretence by deliberately not seeing certain letters on the test chart on the wall. So, I was issued a pair of glasses to help with what I demonstrated as bad eyesight. After this, I had to wear them in class every day, and very soon after that, I began to get serious headaches because the lenses were too strong to see what was in front of me. I got rid of the glasses very soon afterwards.

Again, another attempt at everyday disruption and to fool adults into thinking something was wrong with me was when I suddenly began limping dramatically at home and school. We visited the clinic again, and the doctor asked me to walk around the room a few times. I demonstrated my limp around the room for him and my mum. After about three minutes, he said to my mum, "I think it's psychosomatic." On the way home, I asked my Mum what the word meant and if it was serious. She answered that the word meant I had something else wrong with me. Of course, it was serious. Trying to find ways around life's trappings, usually outside of the home, was a cry for help.

The Dead Crusaders

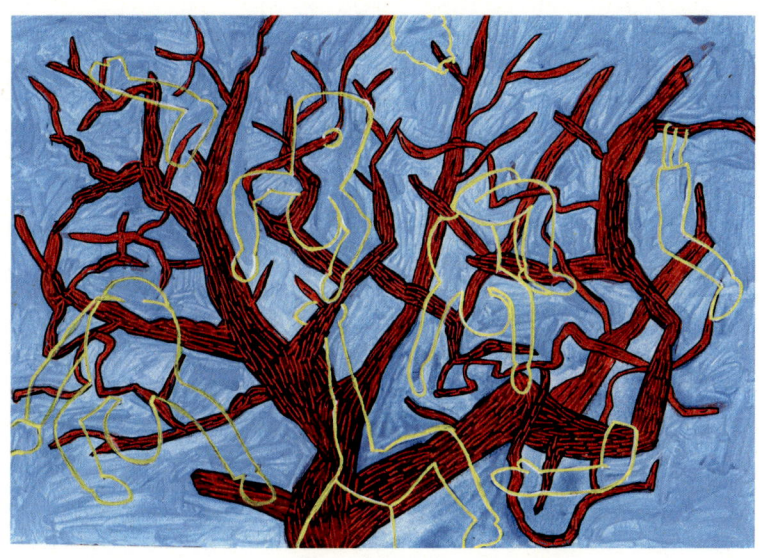

MY FRIEND JOHN LYNHAM'S HOUSE was about four doors down. His was a large Irish family, looked after by Joan, a strong, loving, dominant mother who ran the home. Society would say she was a matriarch. I'm still determining whether the term is positive or negative, but I'll use it as I perceive it: a woman who has earned respect and gained the wisdom to enrich a family or group. Joan was the most serious Catholic in the family. My impression was that the rest of the family were "light Catholics." Dermot, the father, was a labourer who did all kinds of jobs. He was initially hired as a digger, but later worked on the railways and canals in London and Birmingham. More locally, he would be building homes. Whenever I saw him, he would be in his labourer's outfit with mud or dirt all over him, wearing a ragged Yorkshire flat cap.

There was a time when I'd be a frequent visitor in their home, playing games, watching football and wrestling on the TV. They had a small black and white television and various weekend sports. It quietly hummed in the background if no one was watching. One day, I spent an afternoon drawing and painting in the back room with John as boring horse racing was on the TV with the sound turned down. Around this time, I was fascinated with the Crusaders. I was eight years old and loved the pure-looking Templar knights' uniforms. These Catholic warriors emblazoned with their distinctive white mantles with a red cross caught my imagination. Before that day, I would fantasise about being a holy knight, like a superhero battling the world's evils.

Due to the social and emotional impact I was experiencing because of my dad, religion was now viewed with suspicion and betrayal. My love for Crusaders gradually mutated into something else. My feelings towards the Crusaders, who once gave me hope, collapsed into a deep, palpable despair. I spent many hours at night beside my bed, praying for my life to improve. I had hoped Barry would suddenly become a decent human or leave the family. My prayers were not answered, and it all just got worse. So much so his insidious negativity directly influenced my drawings. The Crusaders ended up being impaled onto tree branches and dismembered, bleeding copious amounts of blood, with limbs hanging and bodies scattered on the ground below a large, dark, gnarly tree. There were usually about fifteen to twenty dead of these religious bodies. Joan noticed these drawings as I made them on their lounge table and was deeply disturbed by what she saw. She shouted, "This is the work of the devil!" She then added, "Your father is killing your soul!" and then asked me to leave immediately, as if I was contaminating their home, which I was. I felt contaminated.

Life with Barry was getting more difficult. His dramas were becoming too regular and expected daily. His neurosis flooded out everyone else's emotional and material needs. Everything was raw and sore. I had an animal awareness and was desperately scratching at what seemed like empty space while hanging onto a precarious ledge, just about surviving.

My Best Friend, Bobby

I FIRST MET BOBBY GUTTERIDGE at school at age six. I was sitting with my Mum on a bench in the playground in the morning before the school day began. It was Porters Grange Primary School, and I was new there, starting my education a year later than everyone else because of issues at home. If you were to ask me what these issues were, well, specifically, it's hard to pinpoint, but I'm sure you're getting the gist.

A young black boy with a beaming smile at the opposite end of the playground looked straight at us. He then ran across the playground on the concrete, ignoring all the other children, missing them with his arms wide open. As soon as he reached us, he jumped into my mum's arms and cuddled her. It was a lovely feeling. It was as if we already knew each other. Southend was mainly white in those days, and Bobby was the first black person I had ever met. We immediately became friends.

Bobby had a younger brother named Danny. Both were originally from Ghana and fostered by white Christian parents in their sixties. They were loving foster parents and dedicated to looking after these two young Ghanaians. Rose and Jim may have been Christian, but it wasn't clear whether they were Catholic, Protestant, or similar. Nevertheless, an air of Christianity or its belief was shared through their generosity and love for Bobby and Danny. You could feel a kind of mission in their actions. Their dedication towards the boys was faultless, or at least it appeared that way as an outsider. Bobby and Danny were always positive and got along well with their foster parents.

One memory is that they had a large freezer in their lean-to at the back of the house. They froze everything. Many a time, I was asked to fetch food from the freezer, which could have fitted about eight of me inside.

Private fostering is controversial now, and I didn't know this was what the set-up was with Bobby and Danny. Bobby didn't discuss it much, and neither did his foster parents. From the 1950s to the 1970s, it was common for West African children and babies to be fostered through newspapers and childcare journals.[1] The phenomenon was known informally as farming. West African parents paid thousands of white families to care for their children in the UK. This cultural shift for many Black children was traumatising. They suffered prejudice and abuse, they were singled out, demeaned or spat at by a racist policeman at five years old. Some black kids were treated badly, and others were treated well. It seems like it was a potluck. Years passed before the whole process was questioned. Even at its best, the farming experiment was not the frictionless, emotionally detached arrangement some envisioned. It was messy and confusing. Its legacy is a long shadow that has loomed over the UK's Black African diaspora for almost 70 years.[2]

After school, Bobby and I would fight with other pupils between ages six and seven who hated him because of his colour. I never understood why their racism was so dominant; however, these fights would usually end up as stone-growing jaunts, with either side running away within a few minutes. We were fighting against racists, and even though the context was not positive, it did forge a strong relationship between us. This experience was the first of many battles where struggles against right-wing ignorance and its well-funded ideology were the start of a long journey that has been a prominent factor in my life, and still is, even today.

I used to enjoy staying at Bobby's home at night. Danny and Bobby had separate rooms, which was great. My brother and I shared the same bed at ours, which I hated. Rose and Jim would set up a camping bed for me to sleep on with a sleeping bag, extra covers, and pillows. At night, Bobby and I would share his bedroom. He would be in his bed, and we'd be talking to each other until he would suddenly go quiet and fall into a deep sleep. At times, this fooled me because he always slept with his eyes open, and I'd still be chatting away until I noticed he was asleep. It was an eerie feeling seeing his eyes wide open and not being able to make out the rest of him due to his blackness in the dark. As far

---

1 Why thousands of West African children were privately fostered by white families. *ITV News*. Monday 15 March 2021. https://www.itv.com/news/2021-03-13/the-west-african-children-farmed-out-to-white-families
2 'Farmed': why were so many Black children fostered by white families in the UK? *The Guardian*. Jimi Famurewa. Thu 15 Sep 2022. https://www.theguardian.com/news/2022/sep/15/farmed-black-children-fostered-white-families-uk

as I know, Bobby didn't suffer from any illness. Perhaps as he got older, his eyes began to close.

For a while now, I have wondered where Bobby is. After searching online, I discovered Bobby has been a chef in London for years and seems to have been doing well. In 1993, as Robert Gutteridge, he joined Alfred's as the main chef and had a stint at the Groucho Club. Since 2000, records of his activities as a chef have been more challenging to find. There is a picture of him in his chef's hat, smiling and looking like when we used to know each other. The image is very small and is from the late 1990s, and I cannot find much other information about Bobby online after 2003. There are many friends out there that we have lost in the past and wish to meet again. For me, Bobby is one of them.

Barry's Galleon Ship Disaster

BARRY, MY FATHER, was a man of varied interests and very much into his hobbies. Some of them were illegal. For instance, a few times, he was caught exposing himself in the streets to women he fancied. He sold drugs and was also a pyromaniac. He would often vanish for days and weeks, either because he was in prison or away at a secretive and menacing away day with his black magic group. There are stories my Mum told me about him, where they'd kidnap individuals in a black transit van, but I'm not sure if they're true. There is so much about him that is so outlandishly unbelievable. But, the bits of evidence I know are the events that have materially changed my life. He was a local legend, and his reputation overshadowed the rest of the family.

Whenever we walked around town, it was a strange experience for me, my younger brother, and my mum. Some people who knew about us and Barry's unprincipled activities would keep their distance as if we were about to infect them with a dark, evil curse. Sometimes, it was isolating, like we were pariahs, but at other times, there was an essence of empowerment due to the feeling that people were afraid of us. The problem with being marked as different, scary or dangerous, it attracts types of individuals who find the notion exciting, and when you're a young child, that's the last thing you need.

It was emotionally reassuring when Barry engaged his talents with less insidious ventures. A hobby of his that, now and then, also involved me plane-spotting. He would take me to the airport to watch planes landing and taking off. He watched it all through his binoculars while noting the observed aircraft in his notepad. I was bored, and he was always very excited. His fascination with planes extended to model making. He was extremely proud that he made his model planes from scratch, not assembly kits. He would buy balsa wood and cut it with a craft knife to make model aircraft. He made many different types. Some were painfully intricate biplanes replicating the Wright brothers' first successful aeroplane launched in 1903 and others – WWI aircraft, which seemed less detailed but still revealed high quality and artful technique. These were the moments I remember as special: moments, when he was calm and lost in his craft. He was good at it, and you could feel how enchanted he was by the whole experience.

Another recreation Barry enjoyed was painting. Just like he was obsessed with aircraft in the singular sense, he then shifted much of his creative time to oil painting. His main focus was 16th to 18th century Galleon ships, especially large, multi-decked sailing ships as armed cargo carriers. Again, he was mesmerised by his chosen subject and spent many hours painting different galleon scenes in windy, sea-based settings, with large waves crashing at the side of the vessels. It was all very dramatic. One day, I entered the room as he was painting his latest masterpiece with a slow, intense dedication to detail and noticed all the paintings. I nervously twitched when I saw the problem with all of his galleon works. He was proud of them. I wasn't sure whether to tell him what I had spotted. But I had to. I couldn't help myself. I said the ships had no wind in their sails; they were straight, not as breezy as they should be in turbulent winds. He stopped painting, gazed at all his works, and dropped his arm holding the paintbrush. Barry released a big sigh, and then the room fell silent. He turned round and looked at me with a deep hatred, and it felt like his eyes were burrowing into my skull. He then flipped and smashed all of his canvases. Thankfully, he didn't hit me. He may have been talented at many things, but painting wasn't one of them.

My Dad, Me, and the Genie

MY BROTHER NIGEL and I would be regularly locked in our bedroom for the night by 7 p.m. I remember how bitter we felt towards our parents on Thursday nights because Top of the Pops was about to start on BBC One. We all lived in a rented ground-floor flat, and the front room was next to our bedroom. They didn't have the TV on much, but we could hear it blasting through the wall when Top of the Pops was on. For much of the time, the bedroom felt like a prison where we were both stuck in the room, having to go to the toilet in potties rather than the outside toilet. Even though the proper toilet was situated outside and not inside the flat, it was freezing in winter. At least we had privacy from witnessing each other's nightly defecation.

One morning, I woke up after what I thought was a nightmare. In the nightmare, or what I later came to regard as a real-time vision, I watched my mother and father asleep in their bed in the middle of the night. It was warm, and their window was open at the top, by about four inches. Unexpectedly, I noticed a thick, winding fog slowly slip in through the gap. As it moved into the room, it hovered at the end of the bed. It was a shimmering shadow of a man's body. It floated over to my dad, kneeling on his stomach. He woke up, saw the shady figure, and loudly moaned in fear. The figure began to slap his face repeatedly and wouldn't stop. My father then let out a massive scream, which I could hear in our bedroom, in my sleep.

On waking, I was surprised to see my mother sitting beside me at the edge of the bed, looking concerned. I was still shaking from the nightmare. My mother had her hand on my face to comfort me, and when she pulled it away, it left an imprint, like dark red stains. It looked as if my face had been slapped very hard, but no, there was no pain. The pain I was feeling was my father's, in the memory of the nightmare as it came back to me. It all felt visceral. I could feel fright in my bones. Remembering my dad's face slapped by this entity was unnerving. It was also unsettling to have felt the trauma he had gone through at the same time. I went to school that morning with a red hand mark on my face, and pupils asked if one of my parents had slapped me. Not this time, I said. Whenever we discussed the event afterwards, I would call the mysterious foggy shadow the Genie.

It wasn't until I was in my early teens that I saw *The Nightmare*, painted by the Swiss artist Henry Fuseli. Created in 1781, it depicts a figure sitting on top of a woman – a demon or an imp – while a ferocious-looking horse glares on. The painting draws on folklore and popular culture, simultaneously showing the woman experiencing the vision and dreaming the contents of the vision itself. Fuseli had nightmares like these and, in the painting, put a woman there instead of himself, thus turning it into a personal, gothic fantasy. I'm not sure if the erotic nature of the dream bears any significance for me, although the sensation of fear rings true.

Since then, I've dreamed of shadows in different shapes and sizes. The uncanny thing is that these shadows turned up in my dreams with increasing frequency once my dad had been taken from the uneasy fold of the family. It didn't take long for me to realise that my father was haunting me in my dreams. Not him literally, but first the upset of living with such a chaotic, wild, and dysfunctional father and then him suddenly leaving me, left a massive gap in my psyche. My dreams feature him chasing me, usually in a swimming pool, struggling to swim, trying to escape him. The end would involve us both in a violent struggle in the water and me nearly drowning, but I would wake up just before things got even worse.

The American psychologist James Hillman wrote that the "destructive father destroys the idealised image of himself. He smashes his son's idolatry."[3] He also wrote, "The terrible traits in the father provide a counter education. [...] How more effectively can you awaken moral resolve than by provoking moral outrage at the father's bad example?" These words describe my emotional and strategic response to having two troublesome fathers. As I already said, I have been fighting bullies and the patriarchy my entire life.

---

3   *Fathers and Sons. A Blue Fire: Selected Writings by James Hillman.* Harper Perennial (19 Jun. 1997). P, 220-21.

The Screamer

OUR BEDROOM WINDOW looked onto the back garden, where a collapsed wooden fence provided a rough boundary to an alleyway. The rotten fence merged with the rest of the rough and ready garden weeds and patchy grass. The alley was full of rubbish tipped by neighbours and slack builders over the years and, in places, was overgrown with nettles and a tangle of brambles. However, it was still just about useable for kids wishing to escape their families. We often arranged to meet some neighbouring kids to play games in the street and return home via the alley. It wasn't a secret between us all, but it was like we all possessed an essential morsel of autonomy. Our parents would know where to find us. In the garden, the alley, or outside the house, playing on the pavement.

As usual, my brother Nigel and I were locked in our bedroom for the night. I do not recall discussing it with friends to discover whether it was unusual. We would complain regularly, but it didn't make any difference. It was a strange feeling as if we'd done something wrong and were being punished. But it wasn't obvious what this bad deed might have been, and we were never told. We concluded that they just wanted us out of the way so they could enjoy being together. There were a lot of things going on around this time. My dad was dealing drugs, and they had various friends, which included some who were practising black magic. We would hear their faint conversations in the background whenever their friends came over to visit, but we could never make out what was being discussed.

One night, we were shuffled off to bed, and it felt like any other night with no concern of any troubles looming. But of course, when you least expect it, something leaves an imprint on your dysfunctional psyche. At around two in the morning, I heard scuffling outside in the garden and assumed it was a fox or another animal. We had recently befriended a polecat who used to hang around like a cat, although it would bite now and then. As soon as it arrived, it then suddenly disappeared.

The noise was unsettling enough for me to climb down the bunk bed and try to wake my brother up. There was no stir. Then, I suddenly heard repeated scratching and tapping on the window from outside, followed by strange moans. I slowly moved across the room towards the window to see what was creating the disturbing sounds outside.

It was an older man with a white beard and long white hair. As he saw me, he screamed whilst bashing as hard as he could against the window. He was trying to force his way in. He began swearing at me in between his screeching, angry moans. I screamed at the top of my voice, and he screamed at the top of his, still trying to break the window. The intensity of our screaming at each other was alarming. Those moments were only seconds, but they seemed to be ages and in slow motion, frozen in time. The glass kept us from colliding as if we were both opposite sides of a mirror. Since then, this mirror image has haunted me. It was like he was me in the future, looking at his younger self. We were both shocked at the profundity of the age difference. For me, this future was alien; he was lost and couldn't find his way back home. But as far as my younger self was concerned, he did not belong here.

Thankfully, before the glass cracked in the window, my Mum unlocked the bedroom door and ran in, and then the man ran off into the back alleyway from whence he came. Barry ran into the back of the garden and chased the old guy through the alley. After about twenty minutes, he returned home, saying the older man was swift for his age. Nevertheless, he managed to catch up with him and beat him up.

Shortly after the incident, our parents left the bedroom door unlocked at night, making us feel safer, more trusted, and respected. This decision also helped to lessen the anxiety of feeling captive and not knowing what was going on beyond the bedroom at night, which added a sense of safety.

The experience of encountering the screaming older man has left some scars which have taken a while to fade. One was the feeling of being unable to escape an urgent and potentially damaging situation. This anxiety of feeling trapped is a confusing one because, as I've grown up, there have been various reasons to justify its effect on me. Similar emotions come from different experiences in life. But for years, I have had to contend with fearing being attacked at night by something or someone wanting to hurt me.

I have often wondered who this old guy was and if he was coming around unannounced to try and get drugs while still out of his mind. I also pondered that he was one of my dad's black magic associates who had made a scary mistake while creating a spell or invocation. I do not recall Barry telling me who the old, screaming man was or whether they knew each other.

Years later, Ruth and I were walking past the British Museum when an older man who looked very similar leapt out of nowhere and tried to hit me. He was shouting and screaming at the top of his voice; it was in English, but no one knew what he was hollering. It looked like he was mentally ill and homeless. For some reason, the older man dashed through a small, busy crowd of tourists to find his way to me. He tried to punch me in the face, and I pushed him away and began to hit him in the face, feeling angry. But Ruth stopped me just in time and said that he was just confused and reacting in such a way was wrong; the guy didn't know what he was doing.

Yet, I couldn't shake the notion it was a personal attack and that he somehow knew me, a similar impression to the other older man in my bedroom all those years ago. The deep tensions from the original occurrence returned upon meeting the vagrant outside the museum. It surprised me how potent a distant memory can be. Just minutes of fear in the past can trigger how we react to certain situations. My first and second encounters with these two different older men no longer have the power to dislodge me so dramatically. However, the memories still stir up inner turmoil upsetting the vulnerable child in me. Of course, how these instances affect us are individuals matters, but how we react to them works towards building a fuller being in the world. These experiences shape us differently, moulding who we are and how we engage with others. The fear is personal and can only relate to others to a point. These different moments of childhood trauma have had their journeys within my psyche, where as time goes by, they become more than spectres but informed knowledge that works towards understanding and appreciating others.

Early incidents have created treacherous inner dangers, with wild territories caught in hazy landscapes. Sometimes, one can get lost in them; other times, you change their shape or approach. The key is translating these memories and emotions in ways that are not too upsetting to deal with, with a playful distance. Finding a way to turn them into images and scenarios has made them touchable and less mysterious.

Scars and Toy Rifle Pop Gun

WHEN LOOKING AT MY LEGS TODAY, I can trace those painful moments when Barry viciously placed cigarette burns on them. Domestic violence is a difficult subject to open up about, especially if you're the victim. I have so many different emotional wounds and physical scars backed up inside me. It's like a historical map of abuse. Some cigarette burns are slightly pink but mostly purple crusts as heads, with a dry base on the skin. There are about eight of these small scars, physical reminders of being abused by Barry.

Once, at a GP surgery, I was told directly what they were, and I denied the medical evidence because it was too much to deal with. I just wanted to move on with my life. Whenever friends noticed and asked what they were, I could never give a decent answer. I have always felt too embarrassed and too vulnerable to tell them the truth. But, after years of putting it aside, and since the death of my mum, it feels easier to admit.

I can't recall what his anger was about. Perhaps it had nothing to do with me; he needed someone to lash out at. Sometimes, when thinking back to this moment, I don't feel any physical pain but the haunting memory of the smell of burning flesh. Along with this sensation there is an immense feeling of fear so powerful that I lose my breath.

This happened just before Christmas, so by the time Christmas day arrived, an awful lot of confusion, hate, and fear had welled inside of me towards Barry, who was now enemy no.1. On Christmas morning, my younger brother Nigel, myself, mum, and dad gathered in the front room to unwrap presents together. Barry handed over a pretty-looking wrapped present, which I took from him and unwrapped. It was a toy rifle pop gun. It had plastic bullets, which were quite hard. I loaded the gun, and Barry moved over to me to cuddle me. But before he reached me, I shot a round of bullets into his face. He screamed in pain, and I sat there watching, feeling a mixture of high anxiety and a warm sensation of happiness. For a moment, I knew what it was like to experience revenge. However, the empowerment lasted for seconds as he responded by slapping me hard on my face, which was the main way of hitting me. But it was worth it.

The above image illustrates what I was going through. The title *People Inhabit Other People* literally describes what was happening. It's awful to have someone hold your soul prisoner according to their whims. Whether it's because of religion, dominance, or any other excuse, there is no justification for it. It's like being a slave to someone else's emotionally controlling indoctrination.

Barry the Spider: Out of the Picture

THE DRAWING EXEMPLIFIES the kind of art I made when I was seven and eight. The spidery-looking person is my dad, Barry. The scribbles overlaying him represent me wishing him to be erased from my life.

Black Magic, A Miscarriage, and Horror

MY MOST POTENT TRAUMAS have come from violence and various levels of fear caused by my two fathers, everyday class-related struggles, misogyny, and the constant battle for survival. Just existing was a daily battle. The continuous existential feeling of dread added to the stress and concerns around stability and the disturbing sense of powerlessness resulting from the uncomfortable fact that we were destitute. I used to feel angry and sad that my siblings and I always dealt with this set of conditions. Sometimes, I blamed my parents for much of the mental pain. But, as I got older, I realised many others were also held captive: my next-door neighbours, friends, and many more.

I remember watching the fantastic 1960s classic TV series *The Prisoner*. The protagonist, portrayed by Patrick McGoohan, repeatedly attempted to escape the strange village he found himself captive in and always ended up back in the same place. The series echoed my situation at home and the uneasy connection with the outside world, a mysterious realm of otherness and unknowing. The fifth episode, *The Schizoid Man*, featured Rover, a tool or weapon in the form of a floating white balloon that would incapacitate villagers trying to escape. In one episode, McGoohan, named Number Six, was left unconscious on the beach and attacked by this odd circular menace. This image plagued my dreams, creating nightmares in which I was attacked like a prisoner and then crushed and suffocated. Suffocation was a regular phenomenon in my dreams around this time. I would be squashed into a small nothingness.

My mother, Maria, mostly looked after me, my brother, and my sister on her own. My relationship with her was very close. A strong bond was forged with my mother and brother from the various difficult experiences we shared. Both fathers filled the family's world with endless dramas around their insecurities, affecting the rest of the family. Barry, my first dad, had many strange ideas, habits, and odd friends, and on top of this, he was a leader of a small black magic cult. Their activities would take place outside our home, so I only got information when his friends came and talked to my dad about their weird and troubling experiences. He was a brilliant mathematics student at university before starting a family with my mother. He never had a proper job besides working for the Scotland Yard as a drug dealer and informer. It sounds absurd, but he was like a guru of darkness to a whole group of people. Whenever we visited one of his peers, we would be asked to go into an upstairs room wrapped in aluminium foil. I was too young to understand why, but I now know it was protection from clandestine ears listening in and possible attacks on our brainwaves.

Plenty of other incidents created confusion in my childhood. It was all very stressful. Traumatic situations occurred daily. It was relentless, like living in a constant nightmare. In 1972, when I was eight, Barry was sent to prison. All the drug dealing, family beatings, and mad drug takers trying to break into the flat negatively influenced us. Maria collaborated with Jack, a Scotland Yard detective, to find a way to get rid of him. At the same time, social services took my younger sister Donna from us. To this day, I'm not sure why. I haven't seen Barry or Donna since.

After Donna was gone and Barry was in prison, my mother looked after my brother Nigel and me. A memory from this time has always given me a shudder. At 3 a.m., I was woken up by my mother screaming in pain. I could hear that she was in the front room. I got out of bed and immediately ran in there to see her lying on the sofa in a small puddle of blood dripping onto the wooden floorboards. My younger brother was about five years old and fast asleep, and I was the only person able to help out. Mum asked me to get help. We didn't have enough money to own a landline phone; in 1972, mobiles did not exist. She shouted out that I needed to wake the neighbours for help.

I ran out of the flat and knocked on different local doors, but there was no response. So, I ran to the end of the road to find a call box to ring an ambulance, but I didn't know how to use it. Then I remembered a friend of my mum's called Linda, who was a sex worker and living with her two daughters near the seafront, about two miles away. At 3 a.m., I ran into the red-light district. Luckily, there were not many dangerous people lurking around, and I made it to Linda's front door, banging as hard as I could. She answered. Linda immediately rang the ambulance services.

My brother and I had to stay at Linda's for a few days before Mum recovered and came back home.

On the last night, I slept in the same bed as Linda's two daughters. Nigel slept in another smaller room. They were a little older than me, and it was the first time I had experienced sex. Megan, thirteen and Julia, twelve, were eagerly touching my body in different areas whilst making strange noises. I found the whole episode traumatic and invasive. The surprise of the girls trying out their sexual wares on me while thinking of my mum's pain was all too much. I jumped out of the bed and slept on the floor. When we all woke up, we acted as if nothing had happened. However, Megan was smiling at me across the table at breakfast time. I was shocked by how upfront and confident they were. They seemed much older than their age and worldlier than me. I felt out of my depth and unable to talk at the table, and when Linda said it was time to go home, I was relieved to be leaving.

For years, I was haunted by those memories of running in the streets late at night or early in the morning in the darkness while everyone was in bed. Later, two films reminded me of this feeling. David Lynch's *Inland Empire* tapped into this deep fear of being lost in an alien environment. Laura Dern successfully expressed the unsettling anxiety one feels when alone, running, and getting lost in a dark world beyond one's control where anything can happen. Then there's *Abandoned*, a 2006 horror film co-written and directed by Nacho Cerdà and starring Anastasia Hille. Hille portrays an American film producer who returns to her homeland, Russia, to discover the truth about her family history and gets lost in a nightmarish situation where she faces her doppelgänger in her family home. Both films present us with confused protagonists caught in vulnerable situations whilst experiencing events as if in a dream or nightmare.

When imagining what it's like for people in similar circumstances or war-torn areas or travelling on boats as refugees, my heart aches for them. Being alone, lost in a hostile place, is a form of violence – emotional and psychological. The horror of living in a place and with people where each day is a wait for an event that hurts and confuses creates a hole in the soul. This wounded essence continually tries to heal itself but is interrupted by another unwanted occurrence. How many times can one young individual deal with the repeated onslaught of being caught in the trappings of people's insecurities? Well, let's see.

Head Through the Window

I AM EIGHT, Barry, my mum, and I are in the kitchen. I am sitting on a stool, and they are on their feet shouting. I'm unsure what the argument is about, but it escalates quickly. My dad pushes my mum's head through the kitchen window, and I sit on the stool crying and screaming. The image of her head being pushed through the window has always stayed with me. It's in slow motion, like in a black-and-white movie. Not just that, he didn't just push her head through; he pulled her head back in. Not able to tolerate my screaming and tears, Barry picks up a wet dishcloth and swipes it heavily with force across my face. The power of his whack unbalanced me, and I tumbled off the stool onto the floor. After that, I lost consciousness.

Just as I remember my mum's head going through the window, I can also still remember a painful, stinging, burning feeling on my cheek. I'm unsure how long I was out, but it was probably a few minutes. When I woke up, my body felt extremely sore, and I could feel some of the shattered glass on parts of my body, piercing my clothes and skin. The kitchen floor was smeared with our blood, mostly my mum's. She was sitting with her back against the wall, holding her face. Blood was still seeping out, and I saw shards of glass sticking out of one of her cheeks. My next memory is of us both in an emergency room in a hospital. Barry had broken her jaw. My wounds were fine, and I was patched up with some plasters. However, it took a while for my mum's jaw to heal, and she had to go back to a hospital dentist a few times to straighten some teeth out.

It's an awkward and strange feeling of apprehension when revisiting this memory of myself and my Mum being violently attacked by Barry. I'm unsure, but I think it's the last time I saw Barry. Soon after this terrible moment in our lives, Mum collaborated with Jack, the detective from Scotland Yard and got him sent to prison for over ten years. The intense vulnerability you feel after experiencing your Mum attacked in front of you is difficult to communicate. I can remember that you feel broken, like a snapped twig. Also, there were deep feelings of regret and shame that I wasn't able to defend my mother against this madman. From then on, whenever someone waved their hand near my face, I would suddenly flinch. It was always embarrassing whenever someone noticed my actions because they'd ask what was wrong, and I didn't want to tell them why.

The Demonic Cat

THROUGH THE YEARS, we've had all kinds of animals. I remember we once had a ferret. I do not recall a name, but he joined our family when we had no other pets. He must have had an owner once, and the ferret either got lost or ran away. Males are much larger than females; this one was about eighteen to twenty inches long. He was friendly, very playful, and used to run around like a nutty Jack Russell dog. I can still hear his strange clucking sound in my mind. My brother and I were sad when he finally left us. We didn't see him again.

And then there was Elsa, a Siamese cat and a completely different creature. She was moody and, for some reason, didn't like human males. It seemed to be adult men she had issues with, so my brother and I were safe. Elsa was a very neurotic animal who would always be meowing and running everywhere. One day, we heard a horrible yelping in the back garden next door. We ran out because the sound was so unnerving and saw our neighbour's dog, a male Great Dane, running in circles. On top of him was Elsa, with her claws deep. The neighbours were chasing the dog in all directions. The howling was getting worse by the second as we watched the cat clinging by her claws, looking as though she would never let go. Elsa finally jumped off the poor dog, leaving bloody claw marks on his back. The animal survived, but our relationship with our neighbours was never the same. Thankfully, this was the only time it happened because otherwise, I'm sure Elsa would have been classed as a dangerous threat to other animals and humans.

Mum loved Elsa; they had a strong bond. It wasn't unusual for mum's friends to say that the cat was her familiar. A familiar spirit simply takes on an animal form to aid you, usually as a witch's servant. However, even though the idea was fun, they seemed like close companions. Elsa was protective of my Mum and whenever there were men in the flat, she watched them with suspicion, considering them a threat. Perhaps the cat was responding to the emotional turmoil between Barry and her. The atmosphere was always tense. They were very close, and Elsa followed Mum everywhere. When she wasn't following her, she'd sit on a shelf above the front door of the ground-floor flat. If there were a man at the door, she would pounce on him if he entered the hallway. So, my Mum would check first and then lock the cat in a room before she let the visitor in.

When Ken came along, he'd say they were shit machines and a waste of money. He wasn't really into animals; he was better at killing and eating them. This approach made everything between him and the world much simpler and straightforward. What I've always liked about people's varied relationships with animals is that it can be a possible side step into another way of being. Experiencing a different entity that is not human can bring us into a place beyond the social constructs and everyday trappings of life. Treating them like objects to exploit has never been my thing. Barry tried to like Elsa, but she wasn't interested in him, only biased towards scratching him whenever possible. Ultimately, Elsa was given to another local family, and I hope her life worked out. The irony here is that Mum got rid of Barry very soon afterwards. Ever since then, I have had an affection towards cats.

Happy Family Stage Set

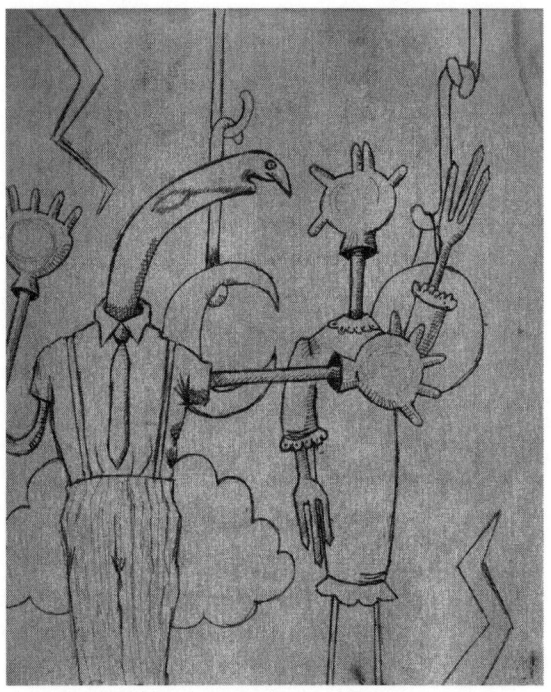

GROWING UP AND WATCHING TV and old movies, the impression of happy families was a strong cultural force, in shows such as *The Brady Bunch* and *The Waltons*. Well, at least that's what it seemed to me. Yet, some TV gems, such as *Children of the Stones*, awoke my curiosity. The setting was Milbury, a village inside a mysterious megalithic stone circle. The series follows the adventures of astrophysicist Adam Brake and his teenage son Matthew. The population are psychic slaves to Hendrick, the local squire, who has discovered the powers of the local stone circle. It felt otherworldly but, at the same time, familiar. The image above concerns the facade of society and the establishment's communication about families.

The Wall of Death

BEFORE WE VENTURE INTO THE KURSAAL and the Wall of Death and my mum's role in its history, I must tell you about her earlier acrobatic antics. She was obsessed with being athletic; her body could contort into various difficult positions, not forgetting her endless cartwheeling. Even though her life was ruled by catholic dogma in the orphanage and its strict rules, her positive defiance was not diminished. She had a lot of wild energy and was a force to be reckoned with. Mum had a variety of flexible positions to show off to peers. When she referred to this period in her life, my mum's impression was of joy, imagination and freedom against the nuns and men running the orphanage, demonstrating a spirit that could not be dominated.

However, accidents can happen when you take risks. At nine, Mum would entertain all the other girls in the dorm with her amazing acrobatics and outrageous contortionism. She would balance on the foot rail at the bottom of her bed, gripping on with her toes. From here, she would turn somersaults forwards and backwards. She would bend backwards and poke her head between her knees. She also told me casually that once she lost her balance and broke her neck, falling off the bed. Ruth reminded me of this memory after my Mum had told her a couple of years before she died. Ruth said, "She told me all this with such glee and a mischievous gleam in her eye. She especially revelled in her memories of the stunned reactions of her fellow orphans." Mum told me her back was in body and neck braces. It took her a few years to get back to the her previous level of agility.

The Kursaal and the Wall of Death are legendary in Southend-On-Sea. Our family lived at Windermere Road, about three-quarters of a mile up the road. The Kursaal was situated on the seafront and spread back quite a way, with a large permanent amusement park behind the main walls. Mum was friends with various people who worked at the Kursaal amusements. I remember the excitement for my brother and me when we were given free entry to some rides; it felt special and exciting. The Kursaal was a community of amazing people; simultaneously, a wild spirit connected all of them. Mum was part of that history from the late 1960s to the early 1970s.

The Kursaal was completed in 1901, with a great silver dome over the entrance. The word Kursaal is German, meaning a "Cure Hall" or spa, and it seems to have been adapted to mean a place of healthy amusement. It was the world's first theme park, pre-dating Coney Island in America. Designed by Campbell Sherrin, who was also responsible for the Oratory, the Kursaal building and its Dome were cutting-edge architectural designs.

Mum rode on the Wall of Death alongside others, some women, such as the then-famous Yvonne Stagg. I cannot remember the main guy who ran the spectacle, but he approached her because she looked sexy and could ride a motorbike. Mum got on well with him but said he was a bit sleazy, trying to get off with all the girls. He briefly replaced "Tornado Smith – once the biggest star of the Kursaal's Wall of Death attraction – who had just died in a South African hospital aged 65."[4] Stagg bought the Wall of Death, took it over and continued to ride herself. In 1974, the Kursaal closed, and Yvonne moved her Wall across the Thames estuary to Margate and a new home at Dreamland, a new Wall of Death venture at 37.[5]

She used to talk a lot about Yvonne, who controlled most of the riders. It was always a scary event for me. I was never allowed to watch my Mum ride the wall, which I was thankful for. But watching the others, including Yvonne, riding the wall was simultaneously spellbinding and scary. I remember my Mum returning home one late evening, shaken after an evening riding on the Wall of Death. While she was speeding around the wall, some of the wooden planks snapped, creating a large hole through which my Mum and the bike slipped through. The next day, Mum bought a local newspaper featuring an image of her bike on the floor. Her fall was luckily cushioned by a dog, which sadly died. After that, my Mum stopped working there and was no longer interested in driving motorbikes and cars. She used to walk everywhere anyway, but this dangerous incident helped make her mind up.

Very soon afterwards, in 1973, the land was sold off for building development, and the Kursaal amusement park closed. We'd walk past

---

4   Mystery around bankrupt Southend Wall of Death legend's £100k. By Emma Palmer. *Evening Echo*, 18th July 2021. https://www.echo-news.co.uk/news/19439250.mystery-around-bankrupt-southend-wall-death-legends-100k/
5   Yvonne Stagg and the Wall of Death: The Queen of Dreamland. *The Independent*. By Lois Pryce, 16 June 2015. https://www.independent.co.uk/arts-entertainment/yvonne-stagg-and-the-wall-of-death-the-queen-of-dreamland-10324541.html

it for years, looking at the rides we used to enjoy, rusting away like a ghost town. So many memories and people's lives fed their energies into this area. However, its downfall was when cheap plane flights to Europe became available, and families shifted their money and holidays abroad. Most of the Kursaal site is far smaller now, with council housing replacing the amusement rides. One of my younger sisters, Samantha, lived there for a while and loved it. Now, she shares a slightly larger home about a mile away with her boyfriend, near our sister Zoe's house, near the council estate we were all brought up on. There was a brief spell when, in 1986, the front building was closed and then reopened. In fact, in 2103, our family celebrated my twin sisters' (Zoe and Sam's) 40th birthday there.

Memories of Place and Drowning

THE WRITER RACHEL LICHTENSTEIN says that place-based writing "today is practised in literature, urban studies, cultural history, anthropology, sociology, geography and other subjects"[6] and the "origins of British place-based writing could be traced as far back as Anglo-Saxon times when poets and scalds (including the female nun Hilda of Whitby, for example) were creating notable works about place and their spiritual worlds." I would say my writing draws on some of the above examples. My mind settles on images and feelings of places whenever I look back.

Place and home affect us in different ways. For example, growing up in Southend-on-Sea, I never felt I belonged there. Mum used to hate it most of the time. She would often complain about how small-minded and racist everyone was. I would challenge her and say that the whole UK is like this. She would respond that London people are much better; they think about things and are not as small-minded, and it is a more diverse culture. It was hard to disagree with her when you're living in a council estate populated by 99% whites, whilst nearly everyone you come across on the street was aggressively staring at you, ready for a scrap. My old friend Bobby, who was black, never visited the estate because he felt threatened in the area. That was fair enough, but I did miss him. Eddie, another black friend, was a foster child like Bobby and came from Ghana; his parents paid his foster parents so he would be educated in the UK. We used to play many games together, such as chess, football and table tennis. But his foster parents moved somewhere else after a little while, and I never heard from them again.

Another danger was more elemental, and it was the sea. Once, I left my Mum sitting on the beach and swam out too far. I went under and began to drift away, eventually losing consciousness. My next memory is waking up on the sand and coughing up seawater. Mum was crying, and I wasn't sure what was happening. Soon after, when my senses returned, I was told that my life was saved by a local man who noticed

---

6   Rachel Lichtenstein. *Estuary: Out from London to the Sea* (Hamish Hamilton, 2016).

me drifting unconscious further out into the sea. I must have been about six or seven then. Another time was when I was in my early teens with my friend John Lynham. We decided to walk out as far as possible, following the tide, which was more than two miles. We reached the water's edge and swam around for a while. We were enjoying ourselves so much that we didn't notice the sudden turn of the tide. As soon as we realised, we started to run back towards the shore. But the water was rising too quickly, up to our chests, and the beach was still too far away for us to get to. The water was rising even faster, so we had to swim to the end of the Southend pier on our left, where we found a rusty, rickety ladder to climb up. Luckily, it's the longest pleasure pier in the world, stretching 1.33 miles. We reached a ladder on the pier's side and climbed onto the wooden platform. John and I sneaked onto the pier's train without paying and rode back to the shore. We sat on opposite seats, shivering and looking at each other. We shared a silence, and I'm sure we both thought we were nearly gone.

    I left Southend about three years ago after my Mum died. I was there with Ruth to be around for her until she left this mortal coil. We used to commute to London to work at the gallery we were running. When I used to walk around Southend, nearly every street had a memory or a few memories where good and bad things happened. So much of my early past, up to the age of twenty-two, returned to me once I lived there again.

A Kick in the Chest

MY FIRST EXPERIENCE OF KEN officially becoming our stepfather was when he suddenly moved into the flat. Mum had been going out with him briefly, but it wasn't long before they decided to make a go of it. They got married at a local registry, and my brother and I, for some reason, were not part of the occasion. It was a big change for Nigel and me to gain a new father so abruptly. I'm not even sure whether it was discussed. It just seemed to happen out of nowhere. Ken knew how damaging my and my brother's acquaintance with Barry was. Observing the narrative between Ken and my mum, the context was that he'd bring some sense of stability to the family. How wrong we all were.

My initial meeting with Ken wasn't the best we could wish for. He sat down in an armchair, and Mum introduced him to us. My brother and I were thrilled to get a new father; he looked fine then. I was so excited that I ran toward him with open arms from the other side of the room, smiling in glee. Before I could get to him and share a cuddle, he swiftly lifted his leg, and his boot sharply thwarted me and hurt my chest. I fell back onto the floor, winded and out of breath. As a warning, Ken expressed some kind of hardman statement justifying his action. That was my introduction. Do I need to say more?

Adopted for a Week

WHEN I WAS EIGHT, after my first father, Barry, was put in prison and we lost my sister Donna to social services, life became a different type of strange. This part of my memory was and still feels mysterious. I visited a psychiatrist weekly for two years. During my visits, I'd be hypnotised and I could never remember these sessions. There are missing fragments of memory relating to this period and the years that preceded it. Yet, I still see some of them teasing me like faint shadows. I can feel them lingering in the distance. But no matter how I try, I cannot determine what they are or what they mean. Through the years, I have had flashbacks, a bit like blipverts. These glimpses are flickering segments of dark moments where I imagine what happened, but I am not sure if any of it is accurate.

I wanted to leave the family because it had become so stressful. Everything felt extremely bleak and harsh. I asked my mother if another family could adopt me. My brother was three to four years younger and didn't seem to be as affected by all the chaotic trauma as much as I was. My mother had successfully disposed of my father, who was the centre of all these issues. Still, even after he had gone, a dark, heavy cloud remained, causing me to feel trapped and depressed. I grimly thought that the family was doomed, like there was a curse on us all. I needed to get out of this prison somehow or spiral into what I believed was going to be a never-ending psychological quagmire of pain and hopelessness.

Our family had become friends with another family, and we got to know them quite well. Daniel and Heather lived on York Road, at the edge of the red-light district. Before we got to know them, my Mum used to go to the café next door to their house. The café was full of all kinds of feral outsiders. Mainly women, who were prostitutes and big, scary, moody lesbians. At least, that is what it seemed like as a young kid at the time. To be honest, I didn't know what a lesbian was. Some would be wearing lumberjack shirts and ragged jeans and short, rockabilly hair, and they had explicit tattoos of sexy women on their arms. Mum met Heather in the café, and they became good friends. I liked the café. It had a completely different atmosphere than everywhere else. It was one of my earliest experiences of a grassroots culture. I wasn't part of it, but I loved its spirit.

Daniel and Heather had two daughters, Maxine and Julia. Julia and I fancied each other; she was a couple of years older than Maxine, and the idea of living under the same roof as them was exciting. Don't get me wrong, Julia and I hadn't done anything physical, such as kissing, although the conversations and games we enjoyed consisted of a mutually intimate energy. I found the spirit of the two girls a fresh alternative to the male violence of my dad. There was a feeling of hope from the whole family and no threats. Daniel and Heather agreed with my mother to adopt me. The authorities would only allow this if they were married, which they decided to do.

I remember being at the wedding celebration in the late afternoon in my little man outfit, black shoes, white shirt and tie. There were about a hundred or more people there. Daniel and Heather made a statement to the crowd about how in love they were and how they had also gained a son. Everyone cheered and clapped, and many people's eyes were on me. It was weird, and I could feel and even see quizzical expressions asking themselves what was happening. I didn't know what was happening either. Yes, I asked to be adopted, but now it was official. It was real. I suddenly yearned that I was lost in the woods or had climbed over a wall and couldn't return home. What a fool I was; what was I thinking?

A few days after the wedding, I moved into their new home with them. It was a big house with lots of light and about four bedrooms. For the first time, I had a room of my own. There were two bathrooms, which I liked, and it felt brand new and spotless. We didn't have central heating or double glazing. Yet, even though the contrast of living in a better home was joyful, I couldn't shake the feeling that I didn't belong there. It was like being in a live sitcom, and I was performing another version of myself. I yearned to be back with my original family again. It was all too scary, and I realised my mother and brother needed me back home. It meant being more robust and more supportive rather than running away. It took me only a week to ask if I could return home. Daniel and Heather were surprisingly accepting of my decision. I was embarrassed about the incident and suspected that Daniel, Heather, and my Mum knew it wouldn't last. I met the girls again another time, and it was as if nothing had happened. We just got on with playing like before.

That inner need to move on was an urge that has stayed with me for years. I am more settled in my later years, but I have always dreamed of living in a different house, city, or country. This desire for change all of the time has taken a long time to simmer down. Responding to what may at first feel like danger or something equally fearsome is a confusing experience. Because now and then, it is the proper reaction. But, with that added sense of fleeing and the need to find a new and safe haven, it is a powerful act of survival and self-preservation.

A Suicide at the Picnic

BEFORE KEN BECAME MY STEPDAD, my mother, Nigel, and I would walk past the local garage where he was a mechanic and chat. I'm unsure how long it took him to replace Barry, our first father, once he was in prison. We didn't miss him, but we did deeply miss Donna, our sister, who was taken away by social services around that time. Everything was rosy when my Mum started to see Ken, and we all enjoyed each other's company. It was before they were married, but he did become our new dad, which was exciting, and we were still living in our ground-floor flat at Windermere Road.

One morning, Ken parked outside the flat in a Bentley T1, which he said was the same type as what the Duke of Devonshire had. I didn't know who this duke was. They put in a picnic hamper in the boot. It was filled with lovely food: rolls, butter, ham, cheese, tomatoes, cucumber, boiled eggs, pickles, etc, and a large crocheted knitted blanket. It was my mum's favourite, and it was zig-zagged. Once inside the car, it smelled fresh with a fully carpeted interior. I can't recall if the seats were leather, but there was a strong smell, which I assume was because they were made of leather. Ken was borrowing it from a friend, Tommy, for the day as payment for repairing the vehicle. It was like a leisurely test run. His friend Tommy was a collector of cars. I remember he once came round in a yellow Lotus Elan. It was fitted with an 8-track tape player, now an obsolete format, playing late 1960s soul grooves.

It was my and my brother's first outing in the countryside. Ken drove the Bentley for about an hour, and none of us except for him knew where we were. He parked us at the top of a hill, and we climbed over a turnstile onto a meadow. Further down was a train line. Mum laid out the large blanket and placed all the food, cutlery, and crockery on top. The sun was out, and there was a light wind. It felt like a perfect day. Boiled egg sandwiches were my favourite. It was one of those rare early moments I remember having with Ken, where we were all happily together, eating and enjoying the moment.

Suddenly, out of nowhere, a policeman began walking up the hill towards us. Ken got up and walked down towards him. They met and talked together, and it all seemed very serious. I wondered whether we had broken the law and trespassed. But this was not the case. Ken returned as the policeman waited halfway down the hill for him. He said that they needed Ken and the blanket; someone had jumped under a train, and the policeman was on his own and needed help to pick up the scattered bits of the body. Mum and Ken stored all the half-eaten food and utensils in the basket. Ken pulled at the blanket, folded it, and walked down the hill. He and the policeman vanished at the bottom, and we could hear police sirens in the distance.

Forty-five minutes later, Ken returned, walking up the hill. His face was grey and green. He was silent and didn't express what he had seen and experienced. We packed everything up, got into the car, and went home in silence.

The Beast

WRITING THIS BRINGS A FEELING of trepidation because of my intense relationship with Ken, my stepdad. Each memory of him is so extreme. It's hard to remember anything other than feeling fearful of him or fighting with him. There are so many stressful moments to write about and to unpack them all as truthfully as possible, emotionally and psychologically, would take another book. However, my chosen examples should give you a rounded picture of what it was like. It's not until recently, in later life, that we have managed to get on. The tragic thing is we only began to find some form of mellow equilibrium between each other at my brother's funeral about fifteen years ago. Mum and sisters asked me to write a eulogy for Nigel, which I did, and when I read it out, he started crying, which was profoundly touching because I knew, as did my brother, that we shared a history of violence and relentless trauma. He said it was the most beautiful and moving thing he had ever heard. Which was a fantastic complement compared to all the contemptuous words he had bitterly thrown at me in the past.

There's only one other time that I witnessed Ken crying. It was one night when he had been out at his local pub. He was back earlier than usual, at about nine. I was in my room, a bit like a studio. I was about twelve. The door flung open, and I was sitting on the floor reading. I looked up at him, wondering what the problem was. Why would he want to talk to me unless I had done something wrong? Instead, he stood above crying, then said, "Do you love me?" I said, "No." He fell silent and stood there shaking with tears trickling down his cheeks. I was cold towards him. In one sense, I assumed that was what he expected, but I did not have the wisdom or emotional capacity to lie and make him feel better. My anger just would not let me. It was a moment of revenge. He closed the door and left me alone to read. At the time, for some reason, it didn't bother me. Days later, weeks later, the memory of that moment kept returning, and a haunting sadness overwhelmed me. The image of him crying, a grown man looking directly at me, a child with so much demand, emotional intensity, and vulnerability, was too much for me to deal with or even understand.

Ken would always force me to protect my brother Nigel whenever he got in trouble. Ken wasn't necessarily bothered about Nigel's well-being. He was more concerned that his family name wasn't tarnished. No one touches a Garrett! Which was a frequent rant whenever anyone in the family suffered a particularly violent incident or was scuffled by anyone outside the family. Again, he would never stick up for my brother and me, and we'd have to deal with the issue ourselves. He was more interested in protecting his blood daughters whenever something demanded his particular skill of brutal angst. He was a fighter, and everyone on the estate was scared of him, which helped us a bit. Local peers who knew about him would think twice before attacking us. However, some saw it as a challenge to themselves to have a bash at a Garrett, meaning my brother or me, or towards our dad in the pub. It was as if we were actors in a gunslinging cowboy movie.

The only cowboy film I liked was *Blazing Saddles,* directed by Mel Brooks (1974), a hilariously zany comedy. I liked how it poked fun at the seriousness of macho men and Wild West cowboy tropes. It was like a bunch of big children acting out silly roles in a Western, but it was a giant playground full of idiots. I also enjoyed its over-the-top jabs at racism and Hollywood. It was a satire of racism, and it showed how stupid racism is. It was groundbreaking. In the 1970s, many kids were excited by Bruce Lee's kung fu films, such as *Fist of Fury, The Way of the Dragon* and *Enter the Dragon*. In the UK, it seemed a bit closer to home because it was a skill where you didn't need a weapon. Although, there were plenty of skinheads and swedeheads walking about with nunchukkas. Judo was my thing. I did a bit of boxing for a while. However, I got chased out of the building and never returned because I unknowingly beat a gang ringleader. You learn that gangs have an etiquette, a rule that whatever the activity, you are not allowed to beat their leaders. I suppose it makes all the little followers feel smaller and less masculine.

On the subject of films, I remember watching *Oliver!* in the 1970s – an adaptation of Charles Dickens's 1838 novel *Oliver Twist*, a 1968 British period musical drama. Two characters had a powerful effect on me; one was Oliver Reed's character Bill Sikes. It hit home how similar he was to my two dads, mostly Ken. The coldness and how violent Bill Sikes was to everyone was like home. And the character Artful Dodger, played by Jack Wild, was me. He even looked like me but in different clothes. Of course, I wasn't a leader of a gang.

Ken employed various approaches to try to make a man out of me. It typically involved me being sent to the Boys Brigade, Army Cadets, Sea and Navy Cadets, and other similar groups. I enjoyed them and learned a lot of things, such as firing guns, radar, fishing knots, sailing, and many different skills. My problem was that even though I got a lot out of learning all of these brilliant and valuable skills, I couldn't take the military side seriously. I found the whole ritual of enacting tough soldiers childish and laughable, and I would be giggling in the line-up as they shouted, "Garrett! What's so funny?"

Living with a tough guy who instinctively lives by the rules of violence as a form of psychological control and as a badge of honour is a scary thing. It's always stressful. Not just for the family but for friends and neighbours as well. When living in the ground-floor flat, we adopted a black puppy. It was always running around, bumping into things, and an extremely jolly animal. One Saturday morning, the dog ran out the front door and accidentally ran into an unhinged and loose heavy iron gate leaning against a wall, and then it fell on top of him. We heard a whining yelp and ran out to see what had happened. The gate was so heavy it crushed the dog's bones in various places. It was excruciating to experience such pain for an animal. Neighbours flooded out of their homes to see what all the fuss was about. Everyone was fretting and shouting about how to help the dog. Ken knew what to do: ran back into the flat, came out with his shotgun, and killed the dog instantaneously, without hesitation. The neighbours, my mum, Nigel, and I stood in shock, silent, not knowing how to react. After all, this guy had a gun.

He had a whole collection of guns; about six out of eight were rifles, along with two shotguns locked up in a wall cabinet. He used to spend hours lovingly cleaning them. These killing instruments seemed more valuable to him than the rest of us did. Sometimes, he dragged me to hunt in the countryside with his pals. The creatures usually hunted were rabbits, hares and pheasants. Ken shared his knowledge of guns and shooting, but I only shot a couple of times. My heart wasn't in it. Later, in the army cadets, I learned how to shoot better and enjoyed it more when using targets, not living creatures. However, I used to pluck pheasants and gut rabbits and hares; it became my job after hunting, which I wasn't keen on, primarily due to the rabbits and hares smelling horrible.

When I was ten, he took me trawler fishing. I never enjoyed it. We would be out very early, about 3 a.m., and sometimes for several days. My main memory is of the wintery cold of the North Sea. It was so cold I could not feel my fingers, and my teeth would chatter. I hated it. My short career as a fisher boy ended abruptly when a large wave bumped the trawler upwards and swept me off the deck into the sea. It was all very quick. As soon as I was in the water, my stepfather's arms reached into the waves, pulled me up, and threw me back onto the deck. He shouted and swore at me. I was not sure whether he was angry with me or worried for me. I think it was both. There were various areas along the South Coast region where my stepfather used to fish. His main fishing crew resided in Old Leigh, an old fishing village in Essex, thirty miles east of London, down the River Thames.

He loved boats. He made them out of wood or fibreglass, and then he would sell them on. Usually, the boats measured twenty to thirty feet. In his retirement, he spent every day at the boatyard building them. When he was a builder, he was one of those guys who would build a house in no time. He also spent much time in the back garden making home furniture. I used to watch in awe as he handplaned wood and fitted legs to chairs and table tops, then lovingly sanded and varnished them. His ideal was to be left on his own, making things; it was one of those things I found magical about him.

Whenever he wasn't making things or working, he'd be at the pub every night. During the week, we were used to him returning home at around half eleven or midnight. One early morning, around 2 a.m., I heard a banging on the front door. I looked out of the front top window and saw Ken leaning against the corner of the wall in front of the front door. I ran down and opened the door to let him in. I assumed he was too drunk to let himself in with his key. But when I opened the door, he leaned on the door frame and nearly passed out. His white, long-sleeved shirt was all covered with blood. The blood's redness was so bright in contrast to the greyness of everything else it zinged. He began to slump to the floor, and I tried to carry this big man from the front door in the hallway into the front room onto the sofa. Being a ten-year-old, I just couldn't manage the task, so he lifted his frame and clumsily guided his body towards the destination. He plopped himself onto the sofa. He said, "Where's yer mum? Go and get her." I ran upstairs and woke her up. She was already awake, and it seemed she didn't want to come downstairs. I shouted that he was bleeding badly, and she still was reluctant and walked down the stairs slowly, as if she was hoping he might die before she got there.

I ran back down into the front room, and on entering, I noticed blood trickling down the back from the middle of his head. On looking closer, I could see a hole about an inch in diameter. I could poke my finger in it. He was losing consciousness, and Mum phoned for an ambulance. The next day, we found out he had been in a fight with other fishermen in the pub, and one of them had a hook and viciously slammed it into the back of his head. Ken was an excellent driver but always drove home from the pub. He usually seemed to get home safely, but it's anyone's guess how he drove home this time. Ken was in the hospital for a few days or weeks, I cannot recall. I do remember that he returned home with a small metal plate inside his head.

    I had learned that the night he got in trouble at the pub, he had heard that his mum had died in hospital. She was in for cancer and fell off the bed somehow and died of suffocation during the night. It wasn't until he had left home that his parents let him know that he was adopted. He didn't know who his birth parents were. However, he deeply loved his stepmum and never got on with his stepdad. He passed down a legacy of male-driven torment to our family, repeating the curse of a stepfather imposing his ways on a stepson. When he first came to join the family, he was fine, but then it got worse. After that evening, when his stepmum died, Ken was never the same again. As years went by, occasional bursts of violence turned into regular moments of terror.

My Entrepreneurial Egg Venture

ALTHOUGH THE IMAGE ABOVE was created years later, it reminds me of an arts and crafts project I made at home when I was about eight or nine. It also reminds me of innocence.

It was a combination of hand-painted emptied chicken eggs placed in straw nests. These special DIY Easter eggs were on sale for two and a half pence each. Once I had made a small collection of them, which fitted into a cardboard box about 40 by 15 cm, it was time to sell them. What better place to sell them than outside our ground-floor flat?

I've no clue what my brother and mother were up to that night and why it was so easy for me to sneak out at about 8.30 pm on a spring evening during the week. I would stand in the middle of the road with my hand up, signalling cars to stop. Most people were polite as they stopped to wind down their car windows as I offered to sell them my imaginative product.

Only a few drivers bought them, but I did sell about four egg nests, making ten pence in total, which I was quite happy with. Then, as I was stopping the next vehicle, I realised it was Ken's car. He stopped, walked up to me and asked what I was doing. I said, "I'm selling my art." He said, fuck that! Get inside. Don't you know how dangerous it is out here at night on your own?

Battle at the Green

WHETHER IT WAS JUNIOR OR SENIOR SCHOOL, it was filled with constant skulduggery and dysfunction alongside small snippets of hope. The struggle of existing in school has been relatively difficult for all kids. I have rarely heard people say school was the best time of their life, even though the popular saying says so. But there are moments of small glory where we can claim personal dignity amongst all the usual confusion and disappointments.

One such occasion was with my good friend Paul Green, a lovely young guy; we used to meet in the morning and walk to school together. He lived on Philpot Avenue, which was not directly part of the council estate like the one we lived on, but still, most everyone there was working-class and struggling to survive. Early morning, we'd meet at the end of my street, Newington Avenue, and wander three miles across Clooney Square, another council estate, to get to Wentworth Junior School. Middle-class people considered it a rough area, but it seemed normal. Our patch of home ground didn't feel that much different.

We must have been about ten years old. When walking to school, we would chat about all kinds of things. One morning, Paul asked if I was gay, and I said I was not sure, but I don't think so. Paul said he thought he was and wasn't sure what to do about it. I asked him if there were any sexual feelings towards male friends. Paul answered not really, but he felt differently towards them and knew something was happening. He was different, noticeably more thoughtful than most other kids. Still, even those qualities weren't enough to define someone as gay. However, we both agreed that he was, and that it was okay. It was our secret.

He was in similar classes as me. One was French, and the class was so chaotic and noisy that the teacher ran out crying, and we never saw her again. In another class, we sat next to each other, and Phil Stanmore, one of the local school thugs who sat at the back, shouted, "You two are fucking queers." At that point, Paul was silent, and I retorted, "You know nothing, you thick shit!" And Stanmore said, OK, prove it. I said why? My disrespectful vibe towards him made him even more aggressive towards me. He ordered in front of the rest of the class that after school, we would meet for a fight on the green, a small roundabout with grass growing on it at the end of the road outside the school. I said yes. I realised I was suddenly defending Paul's honour, not just my own, which felt strange. Yet, I hated bullies, so what the hell.

Paul said he didn't think it was a good idea. At the end of the school day, Stanmore was waiting outside for me. I came out and shouted a few insults and said I'd meet him there. He had a large entourage – or rather, a bunch of sycophants – hanging around him, looking forward to seeing their leader pulverise me. Earlier that day, I had sneaked to the side of the school where there were a couple of skips full of debris from one of the outside huts being refurbished, based in the playground. I lifted out of it a short, heavy plank of wood and shoved it into my school bag. I was scared, but I was also angry. A deep hatred welled up inside me. To me, Stanmore represented everything that I grew up to despise. He was like a younger version of my two violent fathers. He needed to be obliterated with no fuss.

I walked to the green on my own. No one was there singing my praises to support me. For Stanmore, plenty of cowardly voices rang in my ears like chants at a Millwall football match. I saw him standing quietly, he looked surprised I had turned up. I smiled as he began hurling insults at me. But I couldn't hear any of it. Everything suddenly became numb, and my body was shaking at the same time. There were about thirty kids screaming and shouting, fight, fight, fight! Some were shouting go on, Phil, kill him! However, even their voices were faint echoes in the background. I felt very lightheaded, and my body also felt weightless as Stanmore was posturing, performing his dominance for others to view. I swiftly pulled the slab of wood out of my bag and whacked him as hard as I could on the head. I can still feel the hard, dry crack against his cranium. He looked stunned. He was stunned. Like a clumsy rhino, he fell backwards onto the grass. I then ran away, taking the weapon with me. On the way home, I threw it into a bin.

While walking home, I played out various scenarios about what would happen. I was shaking and so scared. Everything around me seemed blurry and distant, and all the traffic, which would normally sound loud, felt muffled. I began to get paranoid that Stanmore's friends or the police were following me, so my legs shifted from a fast walk into a run. On the way home, I chose a different, indirect route through different alleys and roads. Once I was home, I didn't tell anyone what had happened. Later that evening, it was hard to sleep. The humming sound remained in my mind, and it turned into a sharp whistle noise every now and then. I thought I was going mad. But I felt better in the morning and went to school as usual.

Once in the playground, most pupils kept their distance from me and looked at me differently than before. I got annoyed with people because I thought I'd be celebrated for beating the main bully, but during the day, through the grapevine, I heard many thought I had cheated and was a bit of a psycho. From then on, no one bullied me in school. Paul also kept his distance, which pissed me off.

The school, now called Victory Park Academy, is an alternative facility providing full-time education for 101 pupils aged five to 16 with learning difficulties.

Walking Metamorphosis

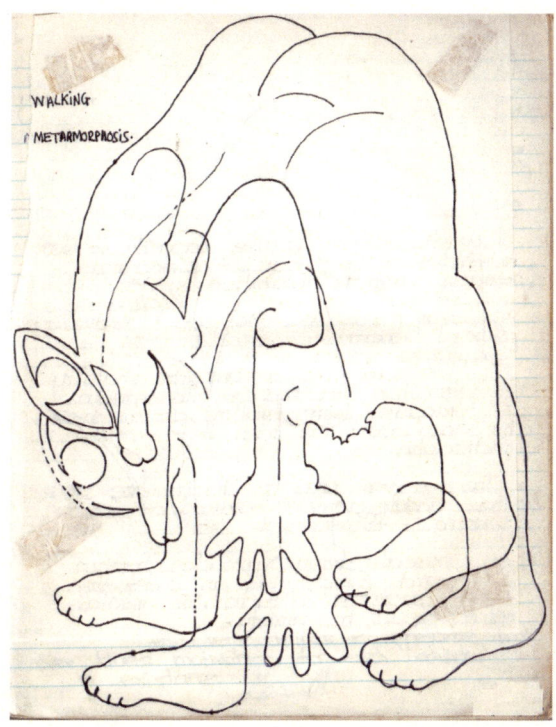

THE INCIDENT WITH STANMORE taught me a few things. When I was fighting him, I wasn't just attacking him. It was a fight against all violent dads, especially mine. It was against what I presumed he was likely to turn into, what he may become. But I was also expressing raw rage in honour of my mother, my brother, and I. It was like moral revenge. Those feelings have always been palpable whenever I have got into trouble. It's like a welling energy that boils inside of me, where my chest feels like it will burst open. An anger overtakes me, and I lose all sense of perspective until that enemy is demolished somehow. The humming sound in my head is a physical factor that buzzes away each time something extreme occurs. I'm unsure if this is unusual. I've always assumed it was a normal feeling.

The *Walking Metamorphosis* drawing relates to the gradual understanding that we are not a single individual but have various inner voices and identities. The anger unleashed that day did not define me in a singular sense. But the fight with Stanmore tapped into a part of me that was tightly wound somewhere inside of me, right until it saw the opportunity to free itself.

From a young age, I've been fascinated with the idea that we are not just one person but we have many personalities. For example, when people say they were possessed or experienced someone else inside them, perhaps many of these were a part of themselves, not usually let out into the world, allowed to rule one's psyche. James Hillman viewed this as an archetypal complexity. Hillman says, "Man is as much in the image of the gods and goddesses when he is ludicrous, enraged, or tortured, as when he smiles."[7] Meaning reason alone does not define us and rule the world, but our mythologies, narratives, emotions, delusions, hate, love, despair, fear, hope, sexuality, pain, loss, death, etc. The Greeks invented gods for these, such as Sisyphus, who, as a punishment for his crimes, Hades made him roll a huge boulder endlessly up a steep hill in Tartarus. We are familiar with Sisyphus being used to represent that part of ourselves, which demonstrates being caught in a non-ending struggle, repeatedly carrying that metaphorical boulder up the hill. Sisyphus is one archetype of numerous entities that helps us see elements and shifts within everyone.

This is why characterisations handed to us by those who rely on singular and two-dimensional public representations to define people do not allow us to explore, respect, and see ourselves and others in more depth. Just think of all the dodgy tabloid press headlines that aim to pull us all into the trappings of the judgement of others with no context, just fear or hatred against someone who does not represent a stunted version of what a human should be. Like a child who never develops or learns, we are taught to be outraged and hurt by others we do not know personally. This limitation is a wound that can be imposed from outside of ourselves.

---

7   Hillman, James. Pathologizing: The Wound and the Eye. *The Essential James Hillman: A Blue Fire.* James Hillman and Thomas Moore. Routledge. 1990. P, 151.

Society can hurt us if we do not challenge its powerful mistakes and endless propaganda, which evolves daily. The irony here is that a lot of public outrage created by the media suffocates our real concerns within, blocking and smothering our vulnerabilities with fake, corporate-orientated emotions. This well-promoted propaganda's raw essence serves only as a condition of hurt on top of fake hurt. Even though we can choose what to imagine – mythologies, folklore, art, tales and images of the past and now –it is still up to us to be aware when they are put in front of us as diversions from us connecting to deeper, essential depths.

Mr Crow

I MET MR CROW three times in my life. The first time was in history class at junior school when I was about ten years old. He was a tall, mild, well-mannered chap who wore the same brown suit every day. As usual, the class was chaotic and noisy, and the poor guy had no chance. He was an academic and must have been scared out of his wits. When he got frustrated with us, he'd shout in a loud, posh-sounding voice. No one took any notice. I wanted to help, but how? I was part of the problem. For example, I made twenty paper planes with other pupils in the class, and we drew a crow head on each. We handed them out to others in the class, and as soon as he entered the room, we all threw the paper crows at him, making crow noises. I could see his face turn red, and it felt like we had broken him. It was one of those moments in life when you hate yourself for being such an idiotic asshole. I couldn't sleep, shifting around in bed, thinking what a bully I was. He was such a peaceful and beautiful person, and I played the role of a bully – the very thing that I was against. It wasn't long before he left.

A few years later, when I was about twelve, I went on a school trip to the Southend Central Museum with other pupils. I was there with others, drawing ancient objects and strange stuffed creatures, when I noticed Mr Crow working there. I hadn't seen him smile before. I'm not sure if he noticed me. But it was a pleasure to witness such a content historian in his element.

Roll on towards 2018. I was invited to a table discussion at the arts organisation Metal in Southend. Mr Crow was also there, amongst others, about twelve people in total. We discussed aspects of fishing history in certain areas of Southend and contemporary politics concerning the town's industry. It was amazing to see him there. I asked whether he remembered teaching at the school, and as soon as I mentioned it, his face turned grey, and he seemed to shudder. I'm glad he found his calling.

Vision On: My Betrayal

AROUND 1974-5, I used to play a lot with my friend Andrew Splain. He was a slightly tubby kid and very bullish. Light-skinned, freckly with a round head and yellow hair, a bit like a young Boris Johnson. You can recognise that his character was selfish and manipulative even at this young age. One example is that he regularly dared people to do dangerous things, such as climb high walls. One day, he was dared back by either me or another friend, and he refused to climb the wall, but we persisted because we had done it ourselves in response to his dare. Once he was on top of the wall, he very soon toppled and fell off and broke his arm. Afterwards, we'd never hear the end of it. He'd claim we forced him to climb the wall. Perhaps we did, but he usually pushed others into doing what they did not want. Soon, a series of small, bitter swipes between each other began.

In the 1970s, there used to be a television program called *Vision On* (1964-76) that many kids loved. Andrew and I also loved the programme and enjoyed making art. He wasn't very good at art but always tried to draw and paint something good. I painted him as a soldier with a hat as a birthday present. He loved it. *Vision On* featured a section on its programme called "The Gallery" every week, exhibiting work sent in by its young viewers. Alongside the artworks chosen to be presented were the name and age of the artist. If you managed to get your work on there, you'd receive a prize, and oddly, no one knew what it was. One day, I was watching my favourite series, and suddenly, my painting of Andrew appeared on the screen. I was shocked because it said that he had produced the work.

It was a painful experience to see my art publicly displayed to millions on television, where everyone thought Andrew had created it, and they did not know it was me. An imposter had pretended to be the creator of my work. To be honest, it wasn't that great of a picture. The head looked like a potato wearing a blond wig with a small mouth resembling a little hole in the face. Not one of my best. However, I did feel betrayed and exploited, which made me feel powerless and empty. Trust and security are questioned when a friend betrays you. Of course, we cannot trust others without the possibility of betrayal. I'm unsure if he knew he wronged me or hurt me. If I was thinking about it too much, I might assume that he was exercising a form of revenge on me while using the situation to gain social status. But I don't think he had it in him to be that devious. Maybe once he owned the picture, he imagined he had created it. The last time I saw him was at a Guy Fawkes night with other families with a bomb fire in the back garden. All I can remember was the enjoyable leisure of eating potatoes baked in foil cooked in the fire in tin foil.

A Wank, the Eleven-plus, and a Circumcision

IT ALL STARTS WITH A WANK, literally. My memory of the wank is lost in distant memory banks amongst a jumble of many other items. But, the result of this wank is of great importance to me because from this moment on, my life got worse and left me to be classed as a lower-than-average individual in society. My age was eleven years, and even though I had experienced elements of it from other people on varied occasions and manners, my sexuality was a rude awakening in discovering how such a thing can influence other factors beyond one's own body. Again, memory does not serve me well regarding how many wanks it took till the moment when cum dried up inside my penis and blocked urine from passing. However, its effect was powerful and led me through a series of situations that were not only humiliating but also disempowering.

    I had trouble passing urine for over a week and could not find the space to tell anyone what was happening, and I felt too vulnerable due to the aggressive climate the family was living in. Tensions were building, and Ken was bullying everyone for any reason. When I went to the toilet to pee, there was an intense burning pain in my penis, and the urine would not come out. It was reoccurring every day, and I hadn't got an appointment with the doctor's surgery until next week. The wait was excruciating, not only because of the pain but also due to the smell of piss on me. I tried to hide it, but it wasn't working. Ken was getting more and more angry with me. His sympathy level was at zero. He began insulting me, saying I was disgusting and I should feel ashamed of the smell and for pissing myself. And yes, I did feel ashamed and also believed that I was the lowest form of scum. I hated myself for what was happening to me and what I was becoming.

    One evening, we were all in the front room watching television, and Ken went on yet another tirade about me and how crap I was. Mum told him to stop picking on me and that he should know better, especially when it wasn't my fault and that it was my current condition. He shouted something like, "the fuck it is", and stood up, intending to hit me. Then, my brother stepped in front of him to stop him, and he was punched in the face. I jumped on Ken to defend Nigel and was thrown across the room, hitting the sideboard. Ken lifted a wooden chair and stood above me, ready to slam me. He abruptly changed his mind and smashed it onto the floor in bits. I was left half-conscious as he left the room, refraining from continuing to inflict any more of his physically damaging outrage on us.

Over the next few days, the immense pain in my penis got worse, and the burning sensation was so conquering that all I could do was lay on the floor screaming. Mum rang the hospital, and paramedics took me on a stretcher to A&E. The doctors examined my penis, and by then, it was swollen and felt like it was about to burst open any second. The next few hours can only be explained as torture. They could not do anything to help my appendage unless all the blood and urine inside were released somehow. A nurse held my penis and began sticking a needle into it, drawing blood. I wasn't given any anaesthetic, and the pain was unbearable. Mum was asked to leave, but because I was screaming so loudly, they couldn't keep her out of the room. She held my hand, crying as I howled like a wounded animal. They were trying to keep me awake as they were stabbing away. But my body wanted to shut down and vanish, close up for the day, after a period of pain which seemed like it was forever. I must have passed out because I woke up in a ward with other patients in beds.

Soon, I was wheeled into a larger ward with other children. I looked under the sheets, and my cock was blood red and very sore, with about fifty small holes. It looked like a deflated balloon. A sorry sight indeed. The next day, I woke up, and it was a warm feeling to be in the company of others of a similar age. That very day, I met a girl my age called Katie. She asked what was wrong with me, and I didn't know how to answer because I felt embarrassed. I'm unsure whether it was that day or the day after, but I was sent to surgery for an operation. I came back from feeling even more sore with what seemed an awful lot of bandages wrapped around my penis. I unpeeled some of the material to see what was left, and the remaining edges of the skin were stitched together. It was hard to make out what was in front of me between my legs; everything was so red. Every day, I was injected in the bottom, which hurt quite a lot. I was supposed to leave the next day, but they held me in for over a week because I was still feeling pain.

For some stupid reason, during my stay at the hospital, the school decided that it was fine for me to take my eleven-plus. To those unfamiliar with the eleven-plus, its name derives from the age group for secondary entry, 11–12 years. It's a way of selecting who's academically suited to attend a grammar school teaching Latin and classical education, deemed a school where oiks from the working classes do not belong. A designated teaching board member, or whatever it was, was watching and timing my exam. I remember sitting in bed feeling pretty out of my mind while writing it. I didn't finish it. I fell asleep. Once I was better and at home, I got my Mum to ask if I could retake the exam, and the school said it was too late and I had failed the test. We tried repeatedly to get them to change their decision, but they would not budge. So, there we go; my future was out of my hands, and I could do nothing about it.

After coming back from the hospital, at first, it was difficult to pass urine, but as days went by, it became easier. Every time I had a bath, I had to add a kind of disinfectant to the water, and they gave me small medical items that looked like golf tees to keep the urethra open gently. It took almost six weeks for my penis to fully heal. However, I still had some embarrassing situations to contend with along the way. One of them was when Mum, for whatever reason, decided to bring Veronica, our next-door neighbour, over to look at my penis while I was in the bath naked. Mum was concerned that my cock was infected and wanted a second opinion before deciding whether to take me to the doctor's surgery. They both agreed that it was not serious. Veronica said, "He's got a nice package; even if he's circumcised, he'll please the girls" They laughed out loud. I asked them to get out, and they did.

Ken didn't apologise for being such a heartless asshole. My bigger concern was failing the eleven-plus. Years later, I would hear political groups arguing about how it was strongly class-biased and that children on the borderline of passing were more likely to get grammar school places if they came from middle-class families. I didn't have much faith in education before my circumcision and the eleven-plus, but from then on, my faith in the education system had taken a deep dive.

Golf and Class War

MY STEPDAD WAS EMOTIONALLY UNGENEROUS and tight-fisted; he never bought anything for anyone. Sorry, that's a lie; he once gave me two quid to buy a plastic football on my tenth birthday. However, he was generous enough to buy a few rounds of beer for his mates down the pub every night. In contrast to his stinginess, Mum would save money from the modest wages she earned while working as a cleaner and at care homes for seniors. She saved money throughout the year with Prudential, an insurance company. Their agents would visit our home and collect money to be saved, and then at the end of the year, Mum would withdraw money saved with interest added. It was especially useful for birthdays and the Christmas period. It wasn't that much, but enough to buy stockings for the end of the bed, clothes, and some toys.

Whenever I visited friends' homes on Christmas day or after, it was noticeable they had more and better-quality presents. Generally, it didn't concern me too much because I would be playing the games with them anyway. I would do the rounds and visit different friends' homes to play with their new toys. These toys included the tabletop Subbuteo football game and Pong by Atari, Inc. One of the earliest video games. In 1976, all the kids got Starsky & Hutch toy cars and bikes in the same colour as the car in the TV series, usually the classic 1970s Raleigh Chopper cycle. But there was that one time when I did steal some of Chris Toops's toy soldiers and felt so guilty that I sneaked them back the next time I went around his house.

Mum was the one who organised our family's move to the council estate. It seems that anything that had to do with organising the family structure or domestics was left to Mum. My stepdad wasn't involved. He worked and earned a wage but begrudged handing over a snippet of his wages to support the rest of the family. However, when it came to his twins, money was a little easier to access for them as long as it was for them and not Nigel and me. He also was a brilliant carpenter and made plenty of chairs and stools for the house. When he was home, he'd either work outside on his car, make furniture, or build a small boat in the back garden.

Whenever the opportunity arrived for me to make some cash, I would jump at it. Being independent was a desire I possessed at a young age. Living on the council estate created new opportunities for earning extra cash. Sometimes, I would walk around the estate alone with a bucket, sponges, cleaning stuff, and wax polish. I knocked on doors wherever there were dirty cars and asked if they wanted a hand car wash. It wasn't much fun, and it felt like begging. So, when my friend John mentioned caddying at the Thorpe Hall Golf Club, I was interested. The golf club resides in one of the richest areas in the Southend.

We would cycle to the Thorpe Hall Golf Club together and stand outside the entrance, waiting to be picked for a caddying job. We both caddied there a few times, but my last time was a harrowing experience, and it left me with an angry and negative opinion about golfers ever since. John and I were walking on the grass, caddying for some golfers, when I heard a distant warning shout, "Fore!". Within seconds, before I had a chance to respond, a golf ball whacked me hard in the chest. I was immediately winded, and I collapsed to the ground unconscious. John said I was out for about forty seconds.

When I woke up, a group of golfing men stood over me. Looking up at all these men was an odd experience, and my chest felt bruised. My eyesight was blurry, and I could hear them discussing what to do. Someone from the group asked if anyone had a chocolate bar in their trousers. A voice said yes, and the guy, who I found out later to be the one who hit the ball, handed me a bar of chocolate. I was still in a daze and took it off him without a thought. At first, I dropped it onto the grass, not realising it was a chocolate bar, and not interested. He suggested I eat it immediately; the glucose would level me out. He picked it up and unwrapped it for me, and still dazed, I grabbed it, said thank you, and took a small bite.

John and some golfers helped me back to rest at the golfing lodge. I was recuperating and waiting for John to return after the golfer he was caddying for had ended his game. About thirty minutes later, he was back with about six golfers, and the one who had struck me with the golf ball had already left. As they sat down in their golfing attire, I noticed their gold watches, their business conversations, and how much money they boasted they were making. On the way home, John said if I hadn't eaten the chocolate I was offered, I could have sued them. I wasn't too sure. Anyway, how the hell was a little urchin such as me going to get it together to sue such a rich, privileged, and respected individual?

The Death of Uncle Don

UNCLE DON WAS A CLOSE FRIEND OF MY MOTHER'S. They had known each other for years. He worked at the amusement arcades at Southend seafront, and his job was fixing all the coin-operated arcade machines. His speciality was pinball machines. My brother and I used to play truant from school and go to his house and play on them for hours, excited that we could play them for free. However, there was another side to Uncle Don, which only became apparent as he got older and his health deteriorated.

It used to feel like a haven away from all the usual home dramas on the council estate and excruciating school chaos and stress. He'd be out working at the amusements if it were during a school day. I spent much of my time alone at his home with library books on art and philosophy, which I didn't understand then. The other thing was that he had a large collection of Readers Digest, which, even then, I found quite conservative, but I still enjoyed reading the content.

Uncle Don also had quite a collection of music. It was enthralling, like a passage into an older generation from a different world. His favourites included Johnny Cash, Ella Fitzgerald, Louis Armstrong, Perry Como, Bing Crosby, Billie Holiday, and Nat King Cole. Most of the songs he played when I was present felt wistful and about loss, with a longing for a world no longer here. My favourite was Ella Fitzgerald & the Ink Spots. Their energy and music felt fluid, upbeat, and poetic.

Sometimes, when I visited him, he would be with a sex worker, Shirley. I think they had sex now and then, but it seemed like they were good friends keeping each other company. A couple of times when I visited, they would be a little drunk and playing strip poker. I remember the playing cards had naked women on them and used to make me feel uncomfortable. Occasionally, I'd play cards with them, but not strip poker and thankfully, they'd put some clothes on. However, most of the time, I'd decline to play cards and made everyone a cup of tea in the kitchen.

I once decided to visit Uncle Don with a friend, Julio. We were walking past Sutton Road near where he lived. We went through the side alley into the back garden, and I knocked on the back door. I had a key and could have let myself in, but I considered it polite to knock instead because I had a friend with me. It took a little while for Uncle Don to answer the door, and when he did, he was naked. He looked dazed, not drunk, but as if he had a fall or something. I asked him if he was alright, and he said yes and that he had just woken up. I wasn't sure. I have seen him naked before on my own and didn't think much of it. This time around, though, Julio was with me, and he was disturbed by the whole situation and was very worried that we'd be sexually assaulted. I told Julio not to worry. It wasn't unusual for my uncle to be wandering about the place naked, and I'd gotten used to it. I asked Uncle Don to put his clothes on, and I made a cup of tea. However, Julio asked if we could go, and I said yes, and we both left.

The last time I saw Uncle Don was when I knocked on the front window. After ringing the bell, he did not answer. Looking through the window, I saw his naked form lying on the rug carpet. I wasn't sure how long he had been there, but I noticed the record player was on and playing continuously at the end. One of the neighbours noticed me outside the house looking through the window and asked what I was doing. I said that I thought Uncle Don inside was dead. They looked in, and when they saw him, they told me to leave and they'd contact the emergency services. They handed me their phone number and said, "Give this to your parents so they can find out what's happening once the police arrive."

I realised that I'd seen a side of Uncle Don that my mother had not been aware that I had seen: the naked side and the strip poker side. I wasn't sure how to deal with Uncle Don. He never threatened me, and he seemed quite gentle and friendly. Later, my mother said that he once tried to sexually assault her in a taxi cab. There was a scar on the top part of her back, which she showed me, and it had been there for years, slowly healing. Mum said he was drunk, apologising the next time they met. He would say that my Mum was the queen of hearts. He loved her. Of course, my mother did not intend to be with him, and he was a bit creepy. Having said this, she did have a side to her where she would take in broken people and support and befriend them. Mum had a generosity towards fallen people, and even though they would be problematic at times, she could forgive their flaws to the point where she could be harmed. Her empathy came from a place of knowing what it is like to suffer; she had experienced deep trauma herself when young and throughout most of her life.

A few years later, Shirley moved to the end of our street on the council estate and didn't look well. She must have been about 50 years old and sometimes would be walking outside her home drunk with hardly any clothes on. When I walked past her bungalow, Shirley didn't recognise me. Instead, she'd shout at passers-by (including me) and swear at the top of her voice. I would ignore her and walk on by. Other locals swore back at her, and many living in the street treated her like a pariah. I was uncomfortable with their demeaning words about her. Shirley was depressed and in trouble, and perhaps I should have made more of an effort to help. Whatever people say about working-class communities, this was not a community.

When looking back and remembering Uncle Don, I now understand at a deeper level how lonely he was. In the UK, societal structures have always been cruel to old people, especially if they cannot afford social support or home help. For years, I wondered what record he had chosen to leave playing. For some reason, I assumed it was *It's a Wonderful World* by Louis Armstrong, which I know he loved dearly. However, that's probably me being all romantic and ironic. The funny thing is, I didn't tell my Mum that I had found Uncle Don dead in his home until years later. Not sure why.

The Great Escape

MY TWIN SISTERS, SAMANTHA AND ZOE, must have been about 18 months old. They were Ken's and Mum's young girls. My brother and I were my first father's and mother's sons. The family had been living on the council estate for about a year, and looking after four children was a big job for my mum, especially when Ken worked most of the time or was down at the pub. I would help by ironing clothes, cooking, and looking after my siblings.

Whenever Ken came home, my brother and I would vanish swiftly rather than experience the usual name-calling, swearing, and bullying. Around six o'clock, either my brother or I would be looking for his white van to pull up outside. Then, we would scatter as Mum was left to do the usual chores. After work, he would be home for dinner, which was expected on the table. He would have a bath and put on a clean set of clothes. I would hide in my room to make art, write or make strange cut-up sounds with broken, second-hand tape recorders. My younger twin sisters were safe because he loved them intensely, and my brother and I were treated as parasites. Unwanted detritus from a different era, from the loins of our blood father, whom he despised. Being there felt like a sin, and we were a constant reminder of Barry daily. By seven, he would leave the house, go to his local pub, and be back drunk at half eleven. It was the early seventies, and everyone was driving home drunk back then.

When Mum decided to escape Ken and go to London with the rest of the family, the decision seemed to come out of nowhere. Yet, it was obvious that it needed to happen, or at least something had to happen. She was trying to save herself and us. Mum couldn't drive. She wasn't even interested in buses; she walked everywhere. Her friend Beryl offered to drive us there. All six of us, with our suitcases, piled into a small car. The raw and nervous energy was a mix of excitement, wonder, and mostly fear. The fear was not only regarding what the hell was going to happen when we got to London. Mum said we were going to visit and stay with her brother Peter. The main concern was how Ken would react. What if someone told him and he chased us on the motorway? Nigel and I kept panicking and looking out of the back of the vehicle, imagining Ken was about to appear and catch up with us in his van. What would he do once he had caught us? It wasn't just the family taking a big risk, but also Beryl, Mum's friend. What would he do to her? Ken was known for his violent temper locally, and even the police preferred to be on his good side rather than bear the brunt of his rage.

Once in London, we went to Peter's flat. We all sat in the car while Mum went inside. She returned after a few minutes, saying the police were there and her brother was nowhere to be found. A police officer returned with her and looked into the car as we gazed back at him with confused, scared eyes. He said he'd contact my Mum soon and we should return to Southend. Mum got back into the car. We asked why he was going to contact her. She looked extremely concerned, and we thought it was because we may have to go back home and worried for Peter. She said that her brother was hoarding stolen goods in his flat and when she visited the police were there looking for him and found her instead. It looked like Peter had decided to leave his flat. It an was unlucky time for Mum. A few months later, she was put in prison for a few weeks by the police.

Beryl and Mum tried to find somewhere else to stay. Mum didn't want to go home that night, worried that Ken would be waiting and feared that he would be in a violent rage. We went to several addresses where Mum's friends lived, but no one was there. It was late evening, and we chanced upon a Salvation Army place for people experiencing homelessness. Hungry and cold, we all stepped out of the car and stood outside the building. Beryl and I had a twin in our arms. My brother Nigel was with my Mum when she knocked on the door. It opened, and a woman in a Salvation Army uniform answered. Mum stepped inside with my brother to ask if they could stay there for the night. Mum returned with my brother, saying they had no room for us. I didn't understand and thought the Salvation Army would help anyone in trouble. I was ill-informed. We ended up sleeping in the car while situated in a car park.

In the morning, Beryl took us back to Southend. The mood in the car was depressing, and we were all very quiet. The deep sadness of going back home was palpable. We stayed back at Beryl's for the day while Mum and Ken tried to work something out. We returned home in the early evening, and everything was fine. No arguments, no tension. However, after a few weeks, Mum was taken from the family fold and put into Holloway Prison. They had not found Peter and suspected Mum was in league with him, even though that was the first time she had tried to meet him in twenty years. She was locked away for about three weeks. Holloway was the largest women's prison in Western Europe until its closure in 2016. The escape failed big time.

Gobbing on the Bobby

I DIDN'T HANG WITH MY BROTHER NIGEL MUCH. One of the reasons was that most of his friends were either violent, thieves, druggies, irritating and more. He was always getting into trouble. One example is when he was dragged home by the police for breaking in and shitting in the local school's swimming pool with one of his pals. We spent our primary years at the school, and one of my younger twin sisters now works in the Infant and Nursery section. I'm not sure if they're aware that her older brother defecated in the same school's pool years ago.

One of the most excruciating experiences while walking around the town centre with Nigel was when we would chance upon a police officer. Gobbing on the back of their coats was a type of dare and sport for him and his pals. First, he would quietly follow the policeman as close as possible and copy his walk, which was already profoundly unnerving. It would last for no longer than a couple of minutes, and then he'd spit on the policeman's jacket. The main prize was not getting caught and feeling smug and that you had one up on the law. There was also a points system. It was simple. Simply managing to spit on a policeman's coat was five points, ten points if it was extra phlegmy, which we called a flob. I was too scared and polite to get involved in his usual shenanigans.

Thinking about it, I think he took after my mum. She always got into trouble at the orphanage and various foster and children's homes in London. In her day, what followed, without fail or question, was violent punishment. Like many in her situation, she was punished as a form of regular discipline, whether any rules were broken or not. Mum rebelled against them anyway. In a way, my brother did, too. Mum and Nigel were wilder than me. I can remember, at times, joking with them that I was the most conservative of us all, other than my stepdad. Although I do not recall him voting, he was your typical working-class Tory. Southend-on-Sea was full of them, and many were into the National Front. Again, even though my stepdad was not affiliated, his views echoed similar tropes. My conservative sensibilities were not political. It was more of a disinterest in mucking about and being pulled into what felt like pointless fatalism. My brother's constant desire to get in trouble was a rebellion that didn't go anywhere for me. Yet, evidently, coming from a feral background has had long-term effects on my life.

She's a Witch!

IN AUGUST 1977, I visited Barbara, a good friend of my mum's. Barbara and her family had become friends when we moved from our dilapidated flat into a larger family home on the council estate. I remember it well because it was the same month that Elvis died. I could never understand what all the fuss was about. The local working-class Elvis fans used to call themselves Teddy Boys, and the younger ones were "rockabillies." Barbara's husband was a Ted, and I used to hate it when he was in because he'd usually be playing Elvis, which I found tedious and old-fashioned. Not just that, like many other skinheads at that time, they were violent and racist. When I visited, he was in tears. He said, "Have you heard? The King is dead!" I thought to myself, good, he's shite.

Barbara wouldn't let me into the house. I guessed it was because her husband needed emotional space to overcome Elvis's death. But I was mistaken; Barbara said I couldn't see them anymore because my Mum was a witch. Not only that, but I was likely to be a proxy with a curse on behalf of my Mum as if she was about to invite a vampire through the door. At first, I found it silly. However, it took a few seconds to realise that others had behaved awkwardly towards us, and we didn't see them socially again either.

Around this time, me and other local kids would meet at Granny Barlow's bungalow at the end of our street. She was a frail old lady. Many of us children on the estate respected her. We would be invited to hers for regular gatherings where she would have an eager audience listening to her folk tales. These visits would last until it was time for us all to go home for evening dinner with our families. In addition to tales, Granny Barlow often shared moments of wisdom. Most of the kids didn't tell their parents about her. It was like a secret we collectively owned between ourselves and hidden from our parents. Soon, some parents found out and told their kids to stop visiting her. A few of us saw her as a kind witch who shared folk tales and knowledge that we would not hear elsewhere. My opinion on witches is that they are outsiders oppressed by the patriarchy, which has been happening for years. It's a feminist and class issue.

Revisiting the Vicarage

> My favourite buildings are all laid to waste. One might as well sculpt a statue from toothpaste.
>
> – Robyn Hitchcock, "My Favourite Buildings"

THE BUILDING MANY OF US council kids frequented locally was the vicarage in the middle of Bournes Green Park, just down the road. In the summer of 1976, the local vicar opened a community area for games at the vicarage, which many of us used. It was a special time when I treasured the experiences of meeting new kids and playing various games. My favourite game was chess, and I had recently beaten my stepdad at the game. He was unhappy about it. In fact, like many sore losers, he threw the board across the room, swearing at me. From then on, I thought there must be something to it. The vicar would regularly bring out these oversized chess pieces made from wood, painted black and white. The pieces were placed onto a large marble chess board outside the vicarage. Each piece was above my knee height. Each move felt more important because of the scale of the pieces, the large, accessible floor surface, and how physical it was. Other kids got bored because I kept winning. So, while occasionally I played solo, I usually had a chess game with the vicar, who was good.

Meeting the vicar was a powerful experience. If you asked me what words of wisdom he shared, I wouldn't remember. My recollection of any words at all from him is not existent. Yet, I do remember his constant instruction and calm, positive energy. No judgment was placed upon my ragged peers or me. He helped me become a better chess player and was one of those rare individuals I had met who was genuine, inspiring and encouraging. He positively affected many of us. There was no other place to go to that resembled a community spirit for kids. It was a safe place, and his being a vicar helped us respect him. Not that any of us scallywags expressed any interest in religion, we didn't. But, a sense of openness combined with a non-imposed sense of order must have positively affected all who came along and participated in outdoor summer games at the vicarage.

This was, of course, too good to last. One mid-afternoon, before I had got ready to leave home and go to the vicarage, Mum gave me the news that some local kids burned the building down. I collapsed in despair, realising that a small light of hope had just been snuffed out. I was handed the local Evening Echo reporting the incident that, as yet, had no information about the culprits. My brother Nigel entered the room, noticing my upset and began to giggle nervously. I asked him why. Mum then shoved at my brother, saying, tell him. He responded by saying no. With a sigh, my Mum said, "He did it!" I said, "What?" Nigel then laughed out loud and shouted, "What if we did? I asked who he had burned the vicarage down with. He, without hesitation, answered, "Richard". It was not surprising that Richard was involved; what shocked me was that my brother was.

It was rare that I would hit my brother, but this, sadly, was one of those times. My anger and despair released an uncontrollable raw energy; it took hold of me, and I punched him in the face. He screamed, and I cried. The sheer disappointment and hatred I felt toward him was something I had never felt so intensely before. The feeling that my brother took part in burning down something so beautiful and real outside of this family. The vicarage was a welcome escape from the usual banality and suffocation of home, school life, and the unending existential nihilism of the council estate. My first dad, Barry, was a pyromaniac. Nigel burning down the vicarage showed it ran in the family. Thankfully, not in me.

How My Art Teacher Inspired Me

I BECAME KNOWN FOR MY ARTISTIC SKILLS on the council estate and frequently drew pets and families, which occasionally earned me a small sum of money and helped me get to know our neighbours. We enjoyed chatting away about local issues and politics. And I enjoyed making the art. Many of the drawings were life-size. I'd be sticking blocks of paper onto their walls so I had a flat and large surface area to work on. I was about 14 years of age then and decided to bring some of this work into the art room and share it with my art teacher and peer pupils. I also brought in other more experimental artworks into the class.

For some reason, my art teacher decided I was an affront to civilisation and, thus, chose to rip up all of my work in front of the class in slow motion, saying, "This – Is – Not – The – Kind – Of – Work – I – Want – To See – In – My – Classroom!" The whole class, including myself, fell silent. My first emotion was that something powerful must be going on in the art I was making to cause such a display of violence. Then, I felt a deep disappointment with my teacher. I thought he was better than this. It also felt like a personal attack.

A fully grown adult being aggressive towards me in response to particular activities was nothing new. It was usually men. One example was my stepfather when I beat him at chess. His response was to hurl the board against the wall whilst directing many expletives at me. I was only 12, and even though winning was a satisfying experience, it was also unsettling. At a young age, older males put themselves in competition with me for reasons I was never sure of. One of the reasons I got on well with females was because I could relax more easily with them. I didn't need to prove myself in any way, we'd just talk about all kinds of things and enjoy shared activities.

My mother was really upset with what happened. The next day, she turned up unannounced and punched the teacher on the cheek, shouting that if he bullied me again, he'd have more than her to deal with. Meaning that my stepfather would visit the school to sort him out. Watching my 5ft 3-inch Mum wallop a man over six foot was quite a sight. It was all very embarrassing. However, I was reassigned to another art class with a different art teacher who happened to be a woman who was much more open to pupils being explorative in class.

This incident could have affected me badly. Yet, it had the reverse effect. I had already been researching at the local library a year before. But it gave me the extra curiosity to make and study more art. I had realised that art was freedom and could open doors into the psyche and emotions that other forms could not do for me. While it felt necessary to possess a certain critical understanding of the world I was growing up in, it also felt essential to allow room for one's imagination to pursue the making of art. From this early experience, I have always felt that there was a war against imagination.

Geeky School Comrades and a Bar Mitzvah

AT CECIL JOINES HIGH SCHOOL, I made some friends who were, like me, geeky. I loved making stuff out of things, pulling things apart, and trying to put them back together again. One example was building my radios from bits of junk found in second-hand shops. These usually involved collaborations with a couple of my school peers. In 1978, David Fox, Frank Couchie, and I built a radio, and the challenge was to get it ready so we could listen to the science fiction comedy series *The Hitchhiker's Guide to the Galaxy,* broadcasting on BBC Radio 4. We didn't make the deadline, but built a working radio. I ended up listening to the series with David on his home radio instead.

David, Frank, and I worked on various projects in the school's physics and technology classes. We finished projects together outside of school hours because we were interested in learning more about how it all came together. One favourite of mine was when we built small air balloons out of wire and tissue paper, propelled by methylated spirits. It was fun to take them to the local park and watch them drift high up in the sky. Usually, they'd either vanish or burn up. Other tasks included testing chemicals with test tubes and mucking around with Bunsen burners. We'd explore this together to build comradeships outside the school's typically rough environment. So, instead of fighting in the streets, we all formed a little club.

We were frustrated with distractions that prevented us from learning. Pupils caused most class distractions, but this was not always the case. I loved learning and was hungry for knowledge. I enjoyed maths and was OK with it, but the teacher, Mr Sage, hated teaching us. His bitterness towards the pupils was palpable, and he always threw his blackboard sponge at anyone in the class who couldn't answer his questions. He would endlessly sigh and shout even when pupils were not playing up. The weight of trying to teach in a hostile environment must have made him lose faith in teaching. A few other teachers were like this, but he was the most aggressive.

Talking about aggression, my battle with Phil Stanmore on behalf of Paul Green still resonated as part of the school's recent history. After his eleven-plus, Paul moved to a different school and area. I never saw him again. Phil Stanmore was more friendly towards me now. However, David was picked on by the usual fuckwits at school, and this made my allegiance to him even stronger. As someone who felt like an outsider and experienced how brutal others can be in my everyday life. My disgust for bullies was as angsty as ever, which was expressed verbally and physically, and it was hard to control. It wasn't uncommon for me to get involved in fights in the playground when pupils were being offensive towards David because of his Jewishness. Many pupils were surprised that I preferred to hang around with those who looked odd or geeky because of my reputation for standing up for myself and coming from a notoriously tough family.

David invited me to his Bar Mitzvah, the coming-of-age ceremony for Jewish boys and girls when they reach the age of 12 or 13. It was an honour to be invited. His parents were open and good-spirited and told me the names of the different types of food laid out on a long table. There were many local Jews present, but only a couple of them were Orthodox. David and his father discussed how their surname was changed by British border security when their family escaped Germany during WW2 because their original name was not easy enough for English-speaking people to pronounce. I ate food I had never eaten before and heard histories that I had only read or watched on TV. This time, it was those who had experienced fascism first hand. The next day, I went to work, and Paul, my boss, who was also Jewish, was interested in how it all went. We had good conversations about Jewish culture that day.

A Slump at the End of the Garden

LIFE IN EDUCATION was a confusing battle and constantly frustrating, and the chaos in school was disempowering. However, I remember gaining some power as a school committee member. The role was about pupil leadership, and other pupils from some of the classes I shared voted for me in my year. I'm unaware of how many votes it took, but I was surprised my peers wanted me to be a committee member on their behalf. Yet, I knew some of them could not be bothered to be one themselves, and others were hoping I'd be of use to them in a dodgy way.

It felt special visiting pupils' classes in my year and asking for suggestions to put forward at the committee meetings. I imagined myself as part of a union, a representative collecting votes and support from peers to change how we were treated by those who ruled. Many of the suggestions could have been more appropriate or attainable. My two main successes were when the board accepted demands for more toilet paper and one day per year without wearing the school uniform. As you can imagine, this was a popular suggestion with pupils, and around this time, it upped my status in the school as a mover and shaker.

It was a strange experience to participate in an after-school committee meeting with other pupils, alongside teachers, where we discussed and voted on which suggestions were deemed workable. What I mean is that pupils were taken seriously and given respect. This was big; I had never received such acceptance from adults before. It was an initiative set up by the new headmaster, Mr Ellington.

I respected and valued one teacher at school, Mr. Crosby, who taught me English. Getting educated was always an uphill battle. I was always eager to learn, but school was always chaotic and full of turmoil and crap teachers who hated the kids. Especially Mr Sage, the maths teacher who always threw a blackboard sponge at you if you got a question wrong. It was stressful. When I was about twelve, I went into an emotional slump. I refused to go to school. This was after I failed the eleven-plus because I had to take the exam while in hospital and was far too ill to finish it. My faith in traditional education after this incident had gone. I felt that it ruined my future.

Instead of going to school in the mornings, I started to go to the end of the garden, stare at the fence, and then close my eyes in despair. Mum tried to help me out of the stink I was in. But no matter what she said, I just sat there in tears. The hopelessness I felt was like a breakdown, although I didn't know what it was back then. All the years of non-stop precariousness, pain, confusion, and anxiety collapsed into one dark slump at the end of the garden. It seemed that there was no point in discussing things. It would have occurred if there had been a chance of life turning out for the better. Whatever I tried to do, I ended up in the same place. No hope and no future. I remember my stomach and my chest feeling hollow, and my head was feeling slightly dizzy and nauseous. I wanted to throw up but couldn't find any content within to spew.

Mum contacted Mr Crosby, who she knew I liked. He visited during lunchtime and sat next to me on the grass. He was still, looking ahead for about ten minutes, not saying a thing. I wasn't crying then, but so much emotion was boiling up inside me it felt like I was going to explode. I wanted everything around me to blow apart into oblivion. Everything was feeling distant and untouchable. It was as if the world and I were ghosts, caught in endless, tedious loops of pain and pointless nothingness. Mr Crosby said, "What's wrong, Marc?" I answered, "Everything, I'm trapped, there's no escape." He answered, "I know, you're not alone." Then he wrapped his arm around my shoulder. Then I cried again for a while. After a while, he left me, returned to the house, and chatted with my mum. About an hour later, I went inside, up the stairs to my bedroom, slept till the next morning, got up and went to school.

How a Library Saved My Life

MY LIFE WAS TROUBLESOME in the mid- to late 1970s at age 13. Our family was constantly under siege, trying to negotiate our dysfunctional ways through the everyday violence at home and on the council estate in Southend-on-Sea, Essex. We also had to contend with intrusions from over-officious social workers. Every route we took led to a different form of disempowerment. The formal education available to me felt worthless and offered no hope for a better future. The general feeling was that we were caught in a hostile system. Unknowingly, we made matters worse. We stole each other's toys, formed gangs, and were always in trouble with peers, neighbours, the police, social workers, and attendance officers.

At this time, the country was almost bankrupt. The Labour government was receiving international loans of $5,000 million and trying to prevent the economy from collapsing. The UK would have fallen into total collapse if not for North Sea Oil. In 1975, the UK's inflation rate peaked at 26%, and unemployment reached the highest levels since WW2. Many companies that had previously been based in the UK and invested in the economy began moving their businesses and assets abroad to more profitable locations. Strikes spread across the land, rubbish was left outside piling up in the streets, and the dead were left unburied. Very soon after this, Margaret Thatcher's (UK's first female Prime Minister) own brand of conservative politics and early forms of neoliberalism would begin to dominate the land.

When I remember these times, my mind usually focuses on what happened to many of my peers after they had left school. A few survived the systemic challenges of bad education and social deprivation. If I used all the fingers on both hands, I'd run out of digits to count how many had committed suicide, died of drug overdoses, or gone to borstal and then to prison. At thirteen, I had a sense of the life I was being set up for and grew determined not to move in that direction. My heart, mind, and soul needed nourishment, and I was not getting it. To change my direction, my behaviour needed to change. So, what was I to do? What decisions needed to be taken to change what seemed hopeless at the time, especially when I was accustomed to feeling disempowered?

Every morning, the day would begin with a long walk into the central area of Southend to the Essex Library. For nearly a year, I pretended I was going to school whilst hiding concerned letters from the school administration sent to my parents about my regular absence. I would enter the library, seeing all the different kinds of people of all ages, researching and reading the abundance of books accessible to anyone. It had a small café then, which was not much of a deal, but going there for breaks I would overhear adults discussing what they were reading. I learned a lot from them and felt I was a part of something special. I read about art, technology, science, religion, psychology, sociology, and politics whenever I was there, which helped create a sense of self-assuredness.

I was shocked that all the knowledge found in this place was not shared with my peers and me at school. It was as if all this information was not "officially" allowed, not for my kind, my class. To say that I was dragged out of the library kicking and screaming once the local council's attendance officer had heard about my antics would be an understatement. The library became my second home. However, my only choice was to return to school or end up in a borstal, which my brother ended up in for couple of years. I knew how bleak and violent borstal would be from friends who had been there. The choice was clear, I went back.

MaThese days, many libraries have closed due to austerity cuts. Much information can be accessed online. However, this differs from the important experience of meeting others in a real, physical learning environment. Moreover, this also goes for education right across the board. If we are forced to rely on online resources alone as a source of knowledge and sharing, future minds will be less informed. Market forces increasingly dominate the Internet, dictating the interfaces/portals and creating bias that privileges corporate values above greater human needs. Libraries provide chance encounters with unexpected sources of knowledge and experience in local community settings.

I owe so much to that Library in Southend-on-Sea.

When Mum Asked Me to Rent Porn from the Local Video Shop

THE FIRST TIME I HAD EVER WATCHED PORN was with my mother, my brother, and Veronica, the next-door neighbour. At the end of Newington Avenue, our street on the estate, there was (and still is) a row of shops on a main road, Hamstel Road. A local family ran a video corner shop, which was always busy. Watching videos at home became a massive trend, and the industry was booming in the 1980s. I left home to earn my income by working full-time at Paul's Discount Clothing Store. Working in a shop paid low wages, but I had enough money to rent a videocassette recorder, which I used at my mum's. I had no television in my flat, just a record player and a tape-playing deck. I got the video VCR to record all the music I liked playing on the TV, such as *The Old Grey Whistle Test*, *The Oxford Road Show*, and *The Tube*. Ken was never about and was usually down the pub with his mates till late.

Veronica popped in from next door one evening and mentioned that she and her husband had watched some porn videos the night before. Veronica said that certain regular members at the local video shop can ask for illegal under-the-counter videos. At the time, porn and video nasties were very popular. A whole new world had opened up, and people wanted to judge for themselves why so much of the material was criticised for being exploitative and consisted of extreme sexual and violent content. I was asked to do the deed and go to the video store. As a member and a local, they knew me and my family, and after a few nods and agreements, I was handed three of the latest videotapes for rent. I didn't know what any of their content was, so it was a gamble, but it felt exciting at the same time.

We watched the infamous video nasty, *I Spit on Your Grave*. We had never heard of it before but later found out that religious groups and feminists reviled it due to its viciousness towards women and extreme violence. We all sat down, not knowing what to expect, and watched uncomfortably as the female protagonist was raped and left for dead.

It all looked so real. I found it hard to stomach and offered to make tea as everyone else watched in shock. After a short period in the film, she rehabilitates herself and takes retribution on her attackers. I can only remember one revenge incident among a few, where she cut off a rapist's penis. Everything in the film was extreme, and we couldn't watch it directly. The sound was turned down, and we all started talking about women taking revenge on scummy, soulless, misogynist males. Then we watched another video which was porn, it featured a policeman and a policewoman having kinky sex, and everyone was laughing because it felt so silly and cliché, which is what it was supposed to be, I think. We also watched another video of a woman having sex with a gun.

I found the whole experience of watching porn with family and friends excruciating. Looking back at it all, I realise that I was the quietest between my Mum and brother and always the most political one, raging against injustices in the world. And when it came to the subject of sex, well, I had no interest in sharing any details or discussing it with them. It was private. Besides, I was still working it all out and didn't know whether I was interested. However, my Mum was obsessed with sex.

There was a paradox with my mum, which was always a bit confusing for me. She hated men overall but came from a violent background and understood violence, and it seems that sex and violence were on the same side of the coin. Growing up with two violent fathers and my Mum saying how she hated them was a strong influence. It turns out that the very males she hated she also found sexy. Some people find violence sexy. James Hillman says that "confidence in male prowess doesn't require talking big"; this can be seen as the heroic combative act of courage. Although, I have never found being a typical cliché that heroic or sexy. I remember all the men at the pubs and clubs leering at women. Some women found it despairing, but many were there especially to enjoy such a situation. You'd also see the same male types picking fights with other men to prove their masculinity to women and their macho peers. The interested women would watch on excitedly, shuddering as the men tried to prove how amazing they were by beating someone up.

I remember when I used to have silver hair and a red Mackintosh, ripped jeans, and scruffy boots. Having insults hurled at me at a disco or anywhere in town in the evening was a regular occurrence. However, coming from a family of tough individuals who were used to physical combat, I would tend to answer back, not with fear but with contempt, disappointment, and hatred. A typical insult from some idiot would be, "What the fuck do you look like? Are you queer or something?" And I would answer, "What if I am? And, what's it to you, you thick cunt!" The result would either be a scuffle or me choosing to swiftly get away once noticing that there were loads of these dumbasses itching to lynch me.

Sadly, Ken was one of those men. Whenever he was out with Mum at a local disco called Totts, he'd end up violently beating up other men who he imagined looked at my Mum for a second or looked different. It was always extreme. Some poor victim would be picked on, thrown through a window, a broken nose, or worse. He thought my Mum found it exciting, but she despised him for it. Mum told me that he was too basic to understand fantasy and took violence far too literally. From then on, I viewed violence by men as a lack of imagination.

Adventure in a Reliant Robin

AT ABOUT FOURTEEN YEARS OLD, I began hanging out with a school friend, Derek Shroud. He was an odd character, which is probably why I liked him. He was obsessed with silent horror films made before the colour era, refusing to watch contemporary films as if they were a toxic threat to humanity's soul. On Sunday afternoons, we'd spend hours in a darkened room watching old classics such as *Dr Jekyll and Mr Hyde* (1920), *Frankenstein* (1910), *The Golem, How He Came into the World* (1920), *The Phantom of the Opera* (1925), *Nosferatu* (1922), and more. All brilliant to watch. However, before the movies were shown on his home projector, he would set up a ten-minute waiting time like in a cinema, playing The Bee Gees in the background, which I didn't enjoy. And then, during the intermission before the next film, he'd play more Bee Gees, argh!

Whenever we sat with his elderly parents for dinner, he was very controlling and would command that they eat slowly and chew about thirty times. He argued in a serious tone that it improved digestion and gave one's body a chance to process the food and absorb nutrients. He was correct but rather annoying, and his parents nonchalantly chuckled at his suggestions, ignoring him. Derek would always act like he was the adult in the room, and everyone else was just playing at existing, so he was more serious and righteous. He ate slowly as everyone else finished their meals and left the table, proving his point. Derek didn't have many friends, but he was happy being on his own and doing his thing.

When Derek invited me to Cornwall with him and his parents, I was surprised he'd asked. Also, I was hesitant. Being stuck in a car on a long journey in the middle of summer with three strangers was not an attractive prospect. However, I had never been to Cornwall, and it would not cost much. I had saved enough to contribute food and petrol, and his parents offered to pay for lodging. As requested, I arrived at their home around five in the morning. It was close to our house, about four minutes away. I wasn't expecting to travel such a long distance in a Reliant Robin. We set off at quarter past five. Derek's parents were in the front, his dad driving, and Derek and I sat in the back. Because the vehicle was so small, we were immersed in bed covers and luggage that didn't fit in the boot.

Our journey to Cornwall had just begun when we had an unexpected encounter with a naked man running along the side of the motorway. There was no other traffic on the road, just this naturist jogger on our left side. For reasons we couldn't explain, Derek's dad slowed the car down to match his running speed, and then his parents conversed with him. He was a skinny man and about six feet tall. They were chatting cheerfully about what a nice day it was. Derek and I could not ignore the man's hairy balls and impressively sized cock bouncing up and down at our eye level. That was the first time I had seen a man's genitalia.[8]

The stay in Cornwall was part of a larger complex at a Butlins holiday camp. That night, Derek was keen on us going to a local disco. I wasn't interested at all, but I went. However, going through the ritual of getting the correct clothes on beforehand was an important part of it all. I hadn't been informed that we would be going to a disco and was not told to bring any specific garments for dancing, so my dress was summer casual. To my surprise, Derek had already chosen an outfit he had brought for the event. It was a dark purple velvet suit. He was insistent, even though it was in the middle of summer, that he wouldn't be too hot. His suit had massive flares, and I felt uncomfortable walking into the club with him. From an early age, my repulsion towards flares was strong. We stayed there for a while, drinking fizzy pop with ice. We were the only young ones in the club. The mistake that Derek made was presuming there would be no adults getting in the way, but as soon as younger kids our age came, they stayed with their parents. Thankfully, the hunt for girls was soon over, and we returned to our shared room and played Scrabble.

---

8 Sorry, that's a lie. I saw Ken's by mistake when Mum and him were having sex in Nigel's bedroom when he was away in Borstal. It was such a shock for me I immediately ran downstairs, embarrassed; they both came down later, giggling and smirking.

The Valentines Card

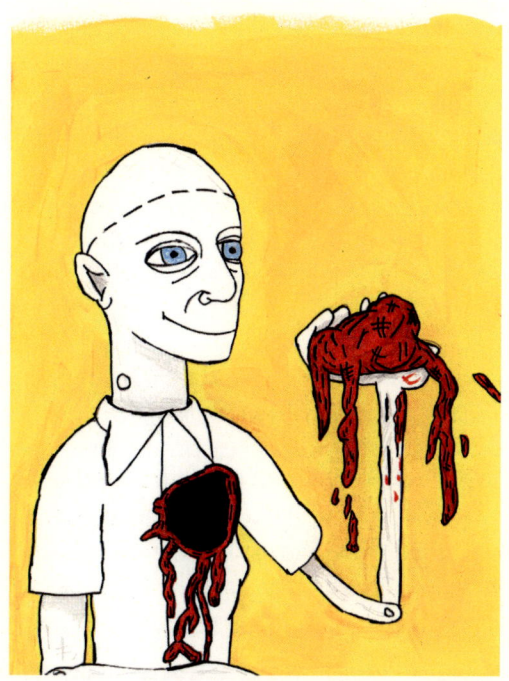

IT WAS VALENTINE'S DAY, and I was about 15. I fancied Lucy North, who was the same age as me at school. We got on quite well, and we had meaningful conversations with each other. I was getting an urge to be with someone who would appreciate me for who I was. Although, in retrospect, I wasn't sure what that was. To assume she would know me was a deluded notion. We enjoyed each other's company and had the same taste in non-commercial, punky, strange music. We especially liked Tubeway Army and Ultravox with John Foxx.

We also shared JG. Ballard books and other dystopian novels. Lucy lent me one book, *Behold the Man*, by British writer Michael Moorcock. It blew my mind. It's an existential science fiction novel about a man who goes back in time and finds out that he's Jesus and is hanged upon the cross. Moorcock was the main writer who influenced many of Hawkwind's songs. Personally, I found Hawkwind and Moorcock a bit too hippy. Yet, *Behold the Man* was a decent book and worth a read.

Since Lucy and I were getting along so well, making her a Valentine's card felt like a fun idea. We seemed close enough that a gesture like that would be fitting. We were also into the fantasy of humans turning into half-robots and cyborgs. The night before Valentine's Day, I put much of my artistic energy into creating a large card for her. It was drawn and painted with a deep passion – perhaps too much passion. The image was a self-portrait of me as a robot (or android) pulling my heart out of my chest and offering the object – visceral and dripping with blood – to her as a gift, a gesture of my love.

I looked around for her in school before the day's lessons and found her in the hallway. I gave it to her, and she smiled and responded courteously. She pulled the homemade Valentine's card out of the envelope and viewed the image with some of her friends while I stood there. She went silent for a few seconds, and so did her friends. Then she said it was creepy and I was sick in the head, and threw it in the bin. Ever since that day, Lucy never talked to me and ignored me. Perhaps she was right to do so. I wasn't happy about it at the time.

Saturday Workers at Paul's Discount Clothing Store

IN THE LATE 1970S, working on Saturdays and evenings after school at Paul's Discount Clothing Store, I met all kinds of Saturday boys. Saturday jobs were common in Southend. The age range was usually between 14 and 18. Paul's father-in-law owned the Army and Navy shop on London Road, about a mile away. It was a family business and his sons worked there. From what I remember, customers thought the sons were always rude. I can vouch for this: they were smug and spoilt. Paul's shop was also a family business, but his son and daughter were young then. I used to babysit for him and his wife, Marlene, now and then. Our shop was generally a friendlier environment and less snotty towards customers.

Because I've worked there since the age of 12, my job was to induct new Saturday workers. Paul and I got on very well, and I enjoyed working there. I loved serving customers and chatting with them about their lives. Taking money at the till was left to the older shop workers, such as Gladys. Gladys was retired and worked part-time. She used to work in finance, was a conservative, and loved Thatcher. Yet, we got on very well. Gladys was an unusual character. She used to keep notebooks that she regularly filled with facts and what she felt was necessary information. She would discuss her discoveries with other shop workers and me, which I found fascinating. She had suffered from polio, and in her later life, its effects got worse. Her neck ached constantly, and her head would shake from side to side. When she first arrived at the shop, her head shaking was a bit distracting, then after a while, I got used to it, so much so that I didn't notice. Ian Dury, the lead singer of *The Blockheads*, contracted polio from a swimming pool at Southend-on-Sea during the 1949 polio epidemic when he was seven. His illness resulted in the paralysis and withering of his left leg, shoulder, and arm.

Gladys hated her husband. We weren't aware of this until Paul and I were invited to his funeral. As the crowd was paying their respects, she broke down in tears and began swearing loudly. Gladys never swore and was usually polite. Unexpectedly, she shouted, "I hated that bastard! He was cold-hearted and used to beat me. I'm glad he's dead!" A couple of her close relatives swiftly came to her aid and comforted her. I left wishing her well. She seemed upbeat at work after the funeral and walked with energy. It was like she had been released from prison.

Working at the shop and meeting people I had not met previously at school and on the council estate was informative. Different classes, different ages, different contexts. There was a Saturday worker named Trevor. He was a confident, middle-class guy with curly, bouncy hair and stood about six feet tall. We often argued about music. He was into heavy metal, such as Whitesnake, Rainbow, Iron Maiden, and Saxon. They were entertaining to listen to, but also felt meaningless – just guys putting on a fake tough act, saying nothing, with guitars as stand-ins for ego and overused rock clichés. It just seemed naff. He found the music I listened to either too political or "a bit gay" (his words). Other than that, we got on well. We used to have fun in the back store room, especially at lunchtime when he, Paul, and I played cricket. We would use scrunched up empty plastic bags secured with sticky tape as cricket balls, while picking up any piece of wood nearby as a bat. The great thing about Paul was that he loved playing about and joking with the staff. He had a big heart. He was quite progressive even though, like Gladys, he voted conservative.

Among many others, one other guy has stuck in my memory. Reg worked as a Saturday boy in the shop and may have briefly worked full-time. He was a troubled soul. Like me, he was working-class and into punk, electronic band Tubeway Army. We used to have quite serious philosophical conversations while eating lunch in the store room. There was an age difference. He was about three years older than me, eighteen. If I recall correctly, I was doing my O-levels at the time. I liked him; something was interesting about him, but I found it difficult to pinpoint what it was. The energy around him felt as if something was looming, about to happen. He wasn't a close friend. But he was intriguing and different, and asked searching questions about life while others around me were not.

Reg explained to me that he was going through difficult changes. He said he thought he was gay but was trying his best not to be. At home, his father mocked and bullied him because of this, among many other reasons. I was sympathetic. I knew what it was like to have my stepfather impose a macho regime on me whilst teasing me because he was convinced that I was gay. After all, I had different politics and ideas, which were not based on typical "bloke mentality." Reg was struggling. He was trapped; it seemed he did not belong to the world, and the world didn't want him. He would talk about suicide, wondering what it'd be like to disappear. He said he would love for all the pain in him to go away. I understood this feeling. I had contemplated suicide at various times myself. Thankfully, I was feeling strong enough to be supportive. Well, I thought I was being supportive. After a few more chats on the same subject, I became concerned that he would do something to himself. His opening up to me felt like a desperate scream for help. I mentioned what was going on with Reg to Paul, and they had a meeting at the end of the working day. Paul was giving me a lift in his car halfway home, and he mentioned he had suggested options for support to Reg, which sounded very positive. So, I was glad I had mentioned it to my boss. However, Reg didn't return to work, so we weren't sure whether he was alive or had found help.

Earlier that day, which in retrospect says much more than I realised then, Reg gave me his copy of "Replicas", the Tubeway Army album on vinyl. It had only just been released in 1979. I was very thankful; it's a fantastic record, and I still listen to it. It was their second album before Gary Numan, the lead singer went solo. For some reason, this LP had a profound effect on me and, like many others back then, it touched me deeply. Numan's dysfunctional and dystopian Ballardian vision spoke to outsiders who didn't fit into society. The lyrics were and still are amazing, expressing raw emotion through electro-punk. Gary Numan got famous quickly and wasn't good at dealing with the public. His robot-like stage persona was later revealed to be linked to Asperger's.

One evening a couple of months later, I met Reg with a gang of rowdy rockabillies in the high street. He was now one of them. He said he was doing fine and had sorted out some of his problems in a carefree, tough man manner. I said that sounded great. His mates were very drunk and shouting for him to tell me to fuck off. They all wanted to get to the seafront and get more pissed. I asked what was he up to that evening. He said, "We're gonna fuck up some queers and niggers." When he said it, he was almost crying. I wanted to hug him and pull him away from those other assholes, but it felt dangerous for me to hang around any longer. So, I said goodbye and walked in the opposite direction, up the high street, to the sound of their shouting and smashing street furniture as they reached Pier Hill.

Jumping in Front of a Bus

THE AGES OF 16 AND 17 were confusing times. Leaving school, searching and finding new versions of myself and operating in the everyday world, asked for skills I had not previously been aware were needed. The journey was an assemblage of wayward, awkward and incompetent steps, grappling with parts of my psyche and the world and not knowing what to do with these emerging life discoveries and situations. I had no guidance.

Another baffling aspect was how to have sex with girls my age. I wasn't scared of them and preferred their company to that of boys. Yet, what I found interesting was the bit where one was expected to perform a sexual act with a young woman friend. I was happy going out to see bands and dancing to electro-music and punk with them. I found the expectation and pressure to have sex immensely confusing, and it felt like it got in the way of intimacy. I'd say from the age of 18, my interest in sex was more positive, yet not necessarily an experience I would desperately hunt for, unlike most other boys my age.

Whenever I went clubbing, especially dancing at local discos in town, I found men – young and old alike – so predictable and cheesy. They'd pose aggressively to girls and strut their stuff. The ritual was always fascinating and very disturbing. These demonstrations of male behaviours were predatory and far too uncomfortably like my stepdad's masculine approach. I found male peers predictable and embarrassing. I was embarrassed for them, not that they cared what I thought. However, I needed clarification about how the behaviours and roles enacted were like stale templates. But, overall, the energy was coming from both sides; males and females were chasing each other. The ritual was all too animalistic for me. Yet, this social conformity was not unusual; it didn't just occur in heterosexual environments. But, with my experiences in punk and new Romantic culture, women were less submissive. Perhaps the truth is that I couldn't be bothered with it all.

The strange relationship with my boyfriend, Jason, was unfortunate for both of us. I wasn't interested in him; I was just exploring a side of myself I didn't know well, and he was my testing ground. I had gone in too deep, and after we had split up, I was relieved it ended. However, it didn't release me from other darker doubts within me. Jason was merely a temporary distraction. At the time, I didn't know if others my age were also feeling the same emotions, thinking about life's deeper meaning, or worrying about the future. I kept thinking that my existence on this planet had to mean something. Why am I here? What's my purpose, and what should I do next?

One night, I was walking late in town on my own. It must have been about 11 p.m. My head was hurting like it had large gripping clamps squeezing it, and it was about to pop. An assortment of emotions swished inside me like a fierce storm, and I needed to turn all the intensity off immediately, like a switch. As I was about to cross the road to the right of me, a bus was about to pass, and I thought to myself, what if I jumped in front of it? Would the pain end? It was weird: almost as if another person was nudging me to give it a go. "Go on, Marc, let's see what happens!" I jumped in front of the bus, and it hit me. I was knocked to the ground immediately. It was a strange one. I lost consciousness and woke up being dragged onto the pavement by a swearing bus driver. As he was screaming and crying, he began pushing, kicking, and punching me. He called me a selfish cunt. I was so dizzy I didn't feel anything. Then, some people pushed him away, and he returned to the bus and drove off.

I was laid to rest upright with my back against a shop window. People asked how I was feeling, and if anything felt broken, I said I was alright. As soon as the bus sped off, I saw people in the vehicle upstairs looking down at me. Many expressed annoyance that I had interrupted their journey. My eyes were blurry and wet from tears, and the lights inside the bus shimmered. The next few days were agonising. I couldn't tell which bruises came from the bus and which were from the driver. But they were not the only pain that hung around for a while. My embarrassment also lingered. I felt like such an idiot. What was I thinking?

Interestingly, the energy that pushed me to do such a thing had occupied my mind for days, as if it was inhabited by an unhappy spirit. It lurked within me. A foggy black cloud took up too much room behind my eyes, causing intense feelings and fuzzy headaches. It was as if it was asking to be let out, pushing me to do whatever it took for it to escape from inside my head, and jumping in front of a vehicle was one of many ways to achieve that. It wasn't long after that incident that I saw someone else walk in front of a bus. They were running across the road, dodging the traffic lights. As the heavy vehicle hit them, I could hear the thud. It was during my lunch break at Paul's Discount Clothing Store and I was going to a nearby shop to get some food. The man died instantly.

My First and Last Boyfriend

FROM AN EARLY AGE, I found it confusing that we conformed to letting our genitalia define our sexual activities and gender roles in society. Kids performed their societal roles, especially in school and on the council estate. Everyone was acting tough and showing either aggression or abusive forms of humour, which usually amounted to less aggressive individuals being bullied regularly. Violence was the currency we all shared. It was everywhere around me, and we were swimming in it. We were always on high alert when playing or just walking around. You could get into trouble if you weren't prepared for anything. For some reason, I was aware that we were being conditioned to exist within a binary world and to not think nor ask questions about gender. I had similar ideas on other subjects and situations, such as poverty and social control. I knew who the villain was, and it all resulted from the same mechanisms dominated by men with too much power. Looking around me, I could see that the patriarchal system was dominating everything, including the air we all breathe.

Because the patriarchy was my enemy, the very notion of it defining me and me being a male confused me. Not only this, the fact that there wasn't anyone around to debate such matters didn't help. I was part of the school's football team. One day, I went to a friend's house, Neil Granger, to prepare for a football match we would play later that morning. He asked if I wanted to put on an oil that soothes muscles onto his legs. I realised that he was testing the ground to see if I was gay, and I was not sure if he was gay or just as confused as I was. Anyway, I refused. Not because Neil unnerved me but because I have always found intimacy with men difficult. I have always trusted women mainly because I have never seen them as a violent threat. Whilst growing up, women have usually been there to save me from men and their fucked-up shit.

After that day, I saw Neil very differently and felt a deep respect towards him. He was different and dared to take a risk with me to see what could happen. That takes guts. I could have been one of those soulless thugs who would spread a rumour in school regarding his (possible) gay antics. But I kept it a secret. I appreciated that he opened up to me;

it didn't threaten my supposed masculinity. Rather, it gave me faith that people were going through all kinds of things, and that our stories needed to be understood, supported, and considered beyond the trappings that forcefully define us.

This leads me to when I was temporarily staying at my Mum's. After some period on a waiting list, my brother was now living in a council flat about three miles away, so the small bedroom was free. I had just left a smelly little bedsit and was waiting to move into a shared house in a few months. I was about 17, and Ken had been kicked out of the house after he had admitted he was having an affair with another woman. Interestingly, this woman looked like his stepmother. Anyway, my seven-year-old twin sisters, my mum, and I were staying together.

During my brief stay at Mum's, I got to know a guy in his forties. His name was Jason, and he used to visit the shop where I worked to buy work clothes. He was a builder and about 25 years older than me. One day, he came to the shop and asked if I was interested in going for a drink one night. I said yes. We met at the Cliff pub, the local gay hangout. I wasn't sure where my sexuality was leaning, but like many young people, I was exploring who I was. His was about 5ft 11, and he was very stocky. If you saw him in the street, you would never assume he was gay. He looked quite scary. He would regularly offer me protection if anyone picked on me. I used to say that I could generally look after myself. However, being young, I must have seemed vulnerable to him. It kind of felt nice that someone was ready to knock the living daylights out of anyone who chose to attack me. However, it was too uncomfortably close to my stepdad, who made it his MO to protect the family with brute violence.

The relationship swiftly turned into something quite traumatic. It only lasted about three weeks, but I had to end it, or who knows what would have happened. Jason became obsessed with me and wanted to see me all the time. Meanwhile, I was still figuring out if I was bisexual, gay or whatever, which frustrated him immensely. He said he didn't care if he could be around me. What helped me to decide to end the relationship was an incident that occurred in the Southend-on-Sea toilets. One night, we were walking along the seafront after the pub. He convinced me to go to the toilets and into a cubicle with him; we entered and locked the door. He immediately began to kiss me on the lips and take my clothes off.

I said I didn't feel comfortable, but he kept pressuring me and continued to take more of my clothes off. I sat on the toilet lid with my pants and trousers pulled to my ankles. He kissed me again, and I found his breath off-putting and pungent. It smelled of cigarettes and beer. I wasn't turned on at all. The situation felt wrong to me. He sucked my cock, but I didn't like it, and I just wanted to leave. It was overwhelming; I couldn't breathe and felt trapped. He realised I was uncomfortable and stepped away, and I pulled my trousers back up. There was a touch of desperation to the whole experience, and he apologised for his sexual aggression. I didn't know how to answer. Jason offered to walk me home, and I said I wanted to go home alone.

The whole episode lingered in my mind for quite a few days. I wasn't sure how I was supposed to respond to the incident. It confused me more than it disturbed me. Perhaps I was too inexperienced. I mean, I hadn't had that many girlfriends and definitely no boyfriends. I had sex by then, but it was still very awkward and unsure. Jason and I met one evening about a week later, and I told him I wanted to break up. We were in a pub in central Southend, which was not a gay pub. He cried loudly and fell onto his knees, shouting that I should give him another chance. The rest of the bar fell silent as fellow customers watched and enjoyed the show. I have always found public displays of emotion uncomfortable. This being a man more than twice my age, it was extra tense. He slammed his fist on the table and walked out. Everything felt so suffocating but once he was gone, I could breathe again.

The next few days were unnerving because he kept ringing me up at my mum's, asking to talk to me. I asked her to say I wasn't in. She didn't pry into what was happening, but I think she suspected it. Every few days, while I was working at the shop, he would stand outside, looking at me with sad eyes. As far as I was concerned, he was the past, and I just wanted to move on. Whenever he turned up and stood outside, I would shudder and shiver as if an evil monster was crawling into my body. It all became scary, and as he continued appearing at unpredictable times, I was getting more anxious. The whole thing seemed to take a sinister turn as I was now being stalked by a potentially violent, middle-aged builder. One evening, I was shutting the shop with Paul, my boss. Jason rested against the railings outside the store, only eight feet away. He was silent, and Paul even asked if he needed any help. Jason answered, "No, I'm fine, thank you," staring at me angrily. After a while, it stopped, and I never saw him again.

Blue Nick

THERE WERE SO MANY FRIENDS and places of interest in Southend for punks and outsiders from the 1970s to the early 1980s. I discovered a curious world beyond home when I left at 15. All my new friends were not from my school but frequented clubs, record shops, clothes shops, and parties. I even met some of them in the street. Every now and then you'd see someone who looked interesting and thought, I must have a chat with them, discuss music and politics. The two main shops that catered to us dysfunctional upstarts were Nasty's and American Graffiti. I met Blue Nick at American Graffiti. I would visit him during lunchtime. We would go to record shops to find the latest underground music and talk about politics, music, class, and other subjects that interest us, such as education.

Nick was in his early twenties, about seven years older than me. The age gap was noticeable; he always said I should go to college and escape Southend for a better life. Nick was the only person I knew who was interested in my well-being in this way. I had done well in my O-levels; he said I should take some A levels. His interest in my life took me aback because we were not that close. He sometimes treated me like a son, which didn't work for me and made it feel a bit awkward. However, I respected his insights. They came from a genuine place.

Mum used to call him Blue Nick because his hair was dyed bright blue. She first met him when he came to collect me from my mum's house on a big, noisy motorbike, dressed in a nun's outfit and big, black leather boots. He was about 6 foot 4, so it was quite a sight. Nick and I were going to the Crocs punk/new romantic nightclub in Rayleigh. I don't know how I got in, I was underage. He wasn't the only one who looked outlandish. I had a long, red plastic mac and silver hair.

After a while, we grew apart. The last time we met, Nick looked very different. He was less New Romantic and more casual and shabbier but still stylish. Nick still had that fatherly tone and told me off. He said I can't believe you're still here. You're wasting away; what's the matter with you? He told me he was leaving Southend and couldn't wait. He was going away to university. That was the first time I felt provincial and that I should work harder at bettering myself and pushing further. I was making art, writing and reading books, but not pushing myself academically. I was still working at Paul's Discount Store.

During my life, I've met certain individuals who have influenced me in a way that niggles at one's psyche. Nick was one of them. He was passing through and leaving me behind in Southend to, potentially, build a decent future for himself. I wasn't aware of it before, but it hit me: Nick was middle class and wanted me, as a working-class lad, to have a better life. When he challenged me, it hurt, not because I felt offended. But because I knew he was right and that I was holding myself back. I began to see and feel my existence in Southend differently from then on. It was as if I had been caught out sleeping and told to wake up. I woke up. I did go to college a few years later to do my A levels and a Foundation art course.

My Brother and Hitler

IN 1980, MY BROTHER was placed in Woodbridge Borstal. Steve, a friend, who was giving us all a lift in his car, waited at my mum's council house for my brother's friend who was also coming. The skinhead turned up at our door and said his name was Hitler. He had a swastika tattooed on his forehead. Mum didn't want to go once she had met him and decided to stay behind and go another time.

It was a torturous journey which mainly consisted of this asshole ranting and raving about how much he hated foreigners and black people. He continued about how the National Front should run this country. This type of individual was (and still is) my enemy. I would normally be fighting him and his sort in the streets with anti-Nazi groups and other allies in Southend-on-Sea or London. We argued most of the way, and even though I had promised my brother I would take him, I shouted to Hitler that he had to shut up or we'd toss him out of the car. My brother was a skinhead but he was not a racist or a bigot. He mainly listened to Ska (Trojan or Blue Beat), reggae, The Specials, The Beat, The Selector, etc. He was just never that great at choosing decent friends.

Steve and I went into the building and saw Nigel first, leaving Hitler outside to wait his turn. I was shocked by how thin Nigel was and the scars and bruises on his face. It felt like meeting a stranger. He spoke very slowly and quietly, almost in a whisper. As soon as we left the building, we ran to the car, leaving Hitler behind once he entered the building. We had promised to bring the scumbag back with us, but we changed our minds without hesitation.

Nigel was released two years later and returned to Southend. He confided in me about some of the incidents at the borstal. His description could have come from the film *Scum*, a 1979 British prison drama directed by Alan Clarke and starring Ray Winstone. It depicts the harsh brutality of life inside a British borstal. When it came out, it was watched by many in the working-class communities across the land. Many people who had, for whatever reason, been put inside a borstal or prison had experienced the scenarios played out in the movie.

The old Nigel never came home; he was replaced with a damaged version of himself. The chipper, cheeky and witty lad had gone. The spirit in him had been replaced with a battered soul. This new person didn't talk as much. He had many silent moods, and his mind would wander off somewhere distant and painful. You could see it in his face. One day Nigel, in confidence, told me that he was attacked by gangs and raped in the Borstal. I wanted to take action and file a complaint, but he was firm about just wanting to move on and leave those awful memories behind.

He moved back to my mums to recover; he really wasn't strong enough to do any physical work. It was like he had come out of hospital after a debilitating illness that he just about survived. Whenever I visited, he hardly talked. Occasionally, he'd talk about football or aliens being spotted near the borstal. He was depressed, and there was a lot of frustration and self-hate welling up inside him. Mum and the twins had to live with him, which was difficult. Every so often, he'd lose it and smash up his room and sound system, sometimes throwing it all through the window, breaking the glass. As I mentioned, Ken wasn't living there during that period. Mum and the twins kept all sorts of secrets from me about Nigel's behaviour. Not for their sake, but for his and probably mine. He was fragile and they thought I'd make things worse by telling him off. He should have seen a psychiatrist or gotten counselling, but we didn't know how to make that happen, and the family didn't trust people who viewed us through an institutional lens. Ours was a typical state of mind: everything that happens at home stays at home.

One day, as I was working at the shop, a friend of mine visited me and mentioned he had found Nigel looking unconscious on the grounds of a local church. I ran to the end of York Road, where the church was and saw him splayed on the ground asleep, not making a sound. Around him were graves and grass of people buried there years ago. I noticed a see-through plastic bag beside him; he was sniffing glue. I lifted and dragged him to a sitting position against the church wall. He was delirious and didn't recognise who I was and began spouting shouts that he had no money and there was no point in mugging him. I explained to him I was his brother, and his eyes looked all grey. He didn't recognise me. I sat and stayed with him, talking about anything so he would become familiar with my voice again. After about half an hour, I managed to get him to stroll back to Mum's with me.

And what of Hitler? Thankfully, I didn't come across him ever again.

Nigel and Fire

I AM STILL DETERMINING what emotional or psychological attributes I have had handed down to me from our first dad, Barry. One of my brother Nigel's worst family traits, inherited from him, was pyromania. Their fascination with starting a fire and burning things down was a powerful attraction that passed me by, thankfully. With Nigel, it was difficult to choose whether it was pyromania or arson. It was both. And Barry was more immersed in the pyromania side, where there was a thrill, pleasure, and gratification alongside a deep fascination with creating fire. He was an extremist and hedonist across the board. Nigel's reasons seemed different, and it was like he was trying to release an awful lot of anxiety, frustration and tension.

Nigel's troubling behaviour found an easy foothold on the council estate, where there were plenty of opportunities and willing accomplices. I understood Nigel's tension; we had both suffered Barry's cruel and selfish behaviours, and now we were under Ken's cold-hearted regime. Whenever 5th November came around, Guy Fawkes Night, parents on the council estate would dread their kids playing with fireworks. I dreaded walking in the streets because there were all kinds of young idiots throwing fireworks at people. This wild, chaotic and typically male activity resulted in scuffles and fights between the throwers and those targeted by them.

One Guy Fawkes Night, my brother and I walked to Thorpe Bay, a much richer part of Southend, and toured the local alleyways. It was about 6 p.m., dark, and freezing. Some Thorpe Bay locals were already in their back gardens, starting fires and blasting fireworks. We would watch different families enjoying the occasion. We never had bonfires or fireworks at home; our parents always said they were a waste of money. My brother and I were both unhappy and jealous watching other kids with richer parents giving them what they wanted. It got too much for us, and we began shouting insults at the happy families from the alleyways. It didn't take long for the police to arrive and demand that we go home, and we did.

Years later, around 1983, my brother was 18, and I was 22. He was recently out of Borstal and I was working at Paul's Discount Clothing Store part-time and at a warehouse for Tony while living in one of his and his wife's (Harriet) properties near York Road. I was there on my own, looking after the house for them, paying cheap rent for a room. I had been there for a couple of months, and to get him out of Mum's house, I invited my brother to live in a spare room upstairs. He was having difficulty finding a place to live, so I helped him out. Tony and Harriet trusted me and left it up to me to make sure the house was fine.

One evening I had been out, and on my way home I could see black smoke drifting in the wind. It was coming from where the house was situated. As I got closer, I could see it was our house. I also saw the fire brigade and police outside, along with my brother and his friend Steve. Water was gushing out of the front door. I asked what had happened, and a policeman said that my brother and his mate had set the upstairs alight by letting off fireworks in one of the upstairs bedrooms. My heart sank. It took a lot of emotional effort to convince Tony and Harriet that their house would be safe under my watch. I felt I had betrayed them by letting my brother live with me. I thought it was inconceivable that he would do something so disrespectful after I found him a home. I sensed that it might have been deliberate, that he did it to hurt me. He seemed to take so much pride in being untameable that I was either gullible or stupid to believe he could behave differently.

After we had been thrown out of the house, Nigel was invited to stay at Mum's council house again. I found another place to live while dealing with being sued by Tony and Harriet. We all agreed to meet at their other house. I intended to convince them it would be a waste of their time and money to try and sue me. They knew they would get insurance but were as shocked and disappointed with me as I was with myself. They agreed that it was probably not a great idea, but suggested I continue working for Tony, and he'd keep some of my pay towards the fire damage. It was about protecting my brother, respecting them, and being honourable.

My brother didn't understand why I was so annoyed and, nonchalantly, said they can fucking afford it. I answered that it was about my work and trust between me, Tony, and Harriet. Nigel then said, in a despairing and bitter tone, that it was far too complicated, and added that I was a fool to trust him. He must have felt guilty somehow, but he wasn't showing it. He was deeply stuck inside his mind, or a part of him was. It was the part I wanted to converse with but it was hidden, seemingly irretrievable. The overall atmosphere around him was that life was empty, alongside a death wish or a disruptive drive to hurt himself badly. The pain my brother had gone through in Borstal and trying to adapt to normal life afterwards made for a dysfunctional and precarious path, riddled with despair and hopelessness.

After about a month, Tony and Harriet decided that we were even. I continued to work at Tony's trophy warehouse on a forklift truck, lifting goods onto vehicles for delivery. Finishing off my A levels part-time at college and working at Paul's Discount Clothing Store was difficult. Yet, my determination somehow gave me the energy and faith to simultaneously study and survive.

Fighting Nazis on a Train

MUM VOTED FOR THE TORIES, which I was against. She voted for Thatcher because she saw her as a strong woman. My family were not political in terms of voting left or right. Like many people, they were not connected to mainstream political arguments, and we were mainly struggling to survive. Also, before Thatcher, the country faced high inflation, and trade unions began to demand substantial wage rises due to the cost of living, which led to what was dubbed the Winter of Discontent. People were desperate for something new to happen.

The right-wing press harshly attacked strikers, and Thatcher's Conservative government introduced major restrictions on trade union power that were extremely effective. The miners' strike of 1984–5 was a defining moment in British coal mining history and the biggest industrial dispute in post-war Britain. It pitted thousands of miners and their trade union against the Conservative government, which supported plans to shut 20 coal pits, causing 20,000 job losses.[9] In 1981 and 1985, significant riots erupted in several cities. The 1981 riots took place in Brixton (London), Toxteth (Liverpool), Handsworth (Birmingham), and Chapeltown (Leeds), while the 1985 unrest occurred in Broadwater Farm (London), Brixton (London), and Handsworth (Birmingham). These disturbances stemmed from long-standing tensions between local communities and the police, intensified by the disproportionate use of 'stop and search' ('sus') powers against young Black men and the worsening economic conditions in inner-city areas, particularly the sharp rise in unemployment.

I'm unsure if as many people would have voted Tory had they known what the future would look like. Still, while the darkness of Conservative ideology swept the land, grassroots culture was finding its voice and reflecting a cultural consciousness of the time. A new type of creative disquiet emerged as an alternative to the mainstream hegemony in the music charts, giving voice to people on the streets. A ragged and untidy

---

9   Miners' strike 1984: Why UK miners walked out and how it ended. BBC. https://www.bbc.co.uk/news/uk-england-68244762

new movement forged its voice within the crumbling infrastructures of a wavering political administration at the end of the Labour Party's demise in the late 1970s and during the Conservative's reign. With its new form of lucid authenticity, punk's arrival declared an awkward expression of disquiet and distrust of the establishment. The disaffected working classes joined forces with the middle classes in a loose alliance to reshape their mutual social contexts.

Other tribes, such as suedeheads and skinheads, pushed a different agenda. Not all skinheads were nasty and racist. Some were part of a musical vibe, dancing to ska and soul with mods and everyday normies. The last burst of multicultural acceptance among skinheads came with 2 Tone music, which blended 1960s-style ska with punk rock. As that genre petered out, Oi! music picked up speed. Oi! was known for combining the working-class skinhead ethos with punk rock energy. Also, to assume that all Oi! was right-wing or even fascist is absurd. Yet, there's no denying that there was a massive right-wing element to all the above. The voices of the left or the non-violent movement were not necessarily widely experienced on the streets. It didn't take long for this primarily working-class movement to be hijacked by a more extreme fascist element connected to the National Front, with neo-Nazis adopting the skinhead look to appear more threatening.

The late 1970s "saw the mod, skinhead and rockabilly subcultures bounce back, partly inspired by the accessibility of punk and partly kicking against it."[10] On bank holiday weekends across the country, seaside towns were crowded with thousands of mods, skinheads, teddy boys, and rockers. Music events often led to fights and riots. Southend has had its fair share of these invasions through the years. I recall one of their chaotic visits when the high street was invaded. From Southend Victoria Station, skinheads assembled in the main square at the top of the high street. Then they all marched down to the seafront shouting Sieg Heil slogans and racist chants. The march was headed by a group of 20-odd skinheads wearing black shirts. The rest – over a thousand skinheads – were wearing National Front gear, swastikas, and National Front letters emblazoned on their jackets. Scuffles and fights were common, usually between punks and skinheads. One Saturday, we had to close Paul's Discount Clothing store

---

10   The Comeback Kids. By Iain Aitch. https://www.museumofyouthculture.com/80s-revivals/

because skinheads were flooding the street the shop was on and smashing everything up, robbing and attacking locals. Arrests were common, and in August 1982, police arrested 21 skinheads in one day.

I've had a few experiences fighting against fascist and racist skinheads. Once, a group of punk friends and I were on a train to London in 1982. We were on the way to an anti-Nazi march. Tensions were building up as we passed each station. On the way, the train began to be populated by skinheads, many from Romford and Wickford. There were about eight of us seated in a carriage. I stood up to go to the toilet and noticed a group of skinheads picking on a black family, mother, father, and two daughters. One of the skinheads slapped the man in the face, teased him, and tried to embarrass him in front of his family. The black guy stayed quiet in his seat, not wanting to endanger the rest of his family. I gave my friends a shout, we attacked the skinheads, and a fight broke out. At the next station, the police entered the train and we were thrown out onto the platform. They left the skinheads inside the carriage with the black family. We all had to wait for the next train to finish our journey to London.

Once there, we rushed to Trafalgar Square and witnessed a group of short-haired, black-shirted guys managing thousands of skinheads, telling them what to do. The anti-Nazi march was gathering many people and it didn't take long for it to escalate into an unhinged, wild punch-up between fascists and anti-fascists. The police allowed the skinheads to disrupt the march, and when people retaliated, they were either attacked or arrested by the police. The lenient behaviour of the British police towards right-wingers, fascists, and racists has always been something that confused liberals and those deemed to be on the left. Strangely, the official anti-Nazi league had dissolved in 1981. Back then, the marches were more violent, but the rhetoric today is just as noisy and angry as ever.

Shoplifting Memories

I PREVIOUSLY TITLED THIS Shoplifters of the World Unite, a song by the English rock band The Smiths, written by Morrissey and Johnny Marr and released in 1987. Morrissey's lyrics endorsed shoplifting and referenced Karl Marx. It's not a literal call to steal from stores but rather an anti-conformist push for spiritual and cultural shoplifting: taking ideas and influences and making them your own. I concur with Morrissey's intentions, but I'm not in agreement with his more recent opinions. People do change, but this doesn't mean what they once expressed is less valid no.

RITA AND JAMES

How can I describe Rita and James? Well, firstly, let's lay down some context. I was 16, it was 1980, I was working at Paul's Discount Clothing Store, and my attire was extremely punky. I met Rita and James at American Graffiti, where punks, new romantics, and other odd types bought clothes that were not sold elsewhere. Rita was an amazing woman with bleached blond hair who was exploring her sexuality to the full with men and women. James was from Liverpool and gay and was frustrated I wasn't interested in sleeping with him. I was really into the music and its grassroots culture, rather than into getting off with people all of the time, which is what they were into. They were wild and full of energy and never scared of getting in trouble.

    I remember spending evenings at their shared bedsit. We would listen to music: punk, electro, gay disco, euro disco, and more. One of my favourite listening sessions was listening to Human League's first album, Travelogue. We just lay on the floor and listened to the whole album in silence. My favourite songs on the album have changed over time. Back then it was "Almost Medieval" and "Empire State Human".

One day, I had my hour-long lunch break from Paul's Discount Store and met them in the high street. Rita suggested that we go shopping for second-hand clothes. We strode off to the biggest charity shop, Help the Aged. We walked around the large shop, separately, browsing for our needs. I found a great top, a bright blue army coat, perfect for wearing that weekend at Crocs, a punk nightclub in Rayleigh, Essex. I waited for them outside for about five minutes, and then they appeared, each with a black rubbish bag full of clothes. James said, "That was easy, they're asking for it." I asked, "What was easy?" And Rita said: "Stealing the clothes." I said, "No way! You didn't." James answered with a snigger, "Oh yes." I was shocked and told them I thought it was low stealing from people who need money. They sneered at me and rolled their eyes like I was not being punk enough, or I was too innocent and wimpy.

Years later, Rita moved to Cornwall. I haven't got a clue what happened to James, and no one I know who knew him knows either. A lot of my friends from the early 1980s have died because of drugs, drinking, suicide, or cancer. Most of them died at a young age, in their twenties. I'm hoping James wasn't one of them.

ROY AND HITCHY SAMUELS

Roy was a good friend and a barber. He was a working-class Jew, very left-wing, and against Zionism. One of his favourite comedians was Alexei Sayle, the English actor, author, stand-up comedian, television presenter, and former recording artist. He was a leading figure in the British alternative comedy movement in the 1980s. These days, Sayle has two programmes on Radio 4: "Alexei Sayle's Imaginary Sandwich Bar" and "Alexei Sayle's Strangers on a Train". I enjoy them both, especially his segment about him hating Keir Starmer. I recommend it.

Roy was married to Jennifer, and they had two boys, aged three and five. They lived on a council estate in Shoebury and were struggling to survive. Even though he earned a salary as a professional barber, he was also a comedian. Roy and I were collaborating on producing political comics. I was the cartoonist, and he was the writer. We co-published two comic books. I loved Roy's sense of humour. It was a great experience working together on "Hitchy Samuels: The World's First Disposable Comedian." The material was raw, comedic punk. The main protagonist was a homeless comedian who was always looking on the bright side of life while philosophising about various experiences that occurred to him.

I would work with him twice a week in their house, usually on Sundays and one evening during the week. He used to play a lot of Steely Dan, which was a bit middle of the road for me, but I got to enjoy some of it. Now and then, Jennifer would come back from Asda's with loads of food, and I mean, a lot. I asked how much it all cost, and she said it cost them nothing. I said how do you do it? She answered it's easy. I just walk out with all of it in a shopping basket with our kids, creating chaos around them and distracting people. Jennifer added, "You must choose your moment, be clever about it, and be calm." It felt exciting that she was kicking against the big companies for survival. I'd never have the guts to do that. Whenever someone tried to steal from my shop, I was happy to catch them because stealing from a small business is much worse. But honestly, it's probably got more to do with if someone is pissing on your patch. It's personal.

I left Southend and didn't do any more punk comics with Roy, and we never kept in touch. We were both as bad as each other in that respect. Years later, in the mid-2000s, I came back to Southend-on-Sea and visited the barber shop where he used to work. While I was getting a haircut from his ex-colleague, I was informed that Roy had a big problem with alcohol. Jennifer left him and took away the kids. Roy was told to leave his job, so he did, and then lost his home and ended up homeless. That was a sad enough story, but to make things even worse I learned he died of pneumonia in the street near where he used to work. He was such an intelligent and positive individual. What a waste of life. The awkward irony of it all is that he became Hitchy Samuels, how uncanny.

GEOFF

Geoff was one of my brother's best friends and he always got in trouble. One day, I met him at Woolworths on Southend High Street. I was on the way out of the shop and walked back to my bedsit on York Road. I heard some shouting behind me and saw Geoff running with a yucca plant. I say, running. It was more of a fast walk. He was chased by security guards. The plant was as big as him, and he was gradually slowing down because it was far too heavy to run with. The security guards caught up with him, taking him back to the shop as other police gathered. I was surprised that he had convinced himself that he'd be able to lift a large plant like that and escape from security.

He had form. Another time, he robbed a flat while a couple were asleep in bed. He successfully stole some items, such as jewellery and left. However, several police officers visited his home, asking if he had lost his wallet. He said yes, and they arrested him immediately. The couple he robbed found his wallet on the floor next to the window where he had broken in. Sadly, poor Geoff just wasn't a very successful thief.

He used to visit my brother at my mum's home in the council estate. If I happened to be there, I would have always been tough on him because Geoff seemed to be a bad influence. Which is stupid because my brother was probably a worse influence on him. Anyway, the last time I saw him was about a year before my mum's death and many years after my brother's when he asked if he could leave a couple of bags under the stairs until he could collect them another time. Mum said yes and was happy to help him. The two bags were full of clothes and a PlayStation with various games. A few months later, we heard that Geoff was killed on the motorway on his scooter on the way to his home in Kent. We were both very sad to hear the news. He had a tough life.

Remembering conversations that I once had with these friends (and other friends and family) who have since left this mortal coil feels quite strange. I've always imagined that they remembered certain discussions we've had at various moments. And yet, when they die, those memories fade away and die with them. Where do these lost memories go?

Silent Command

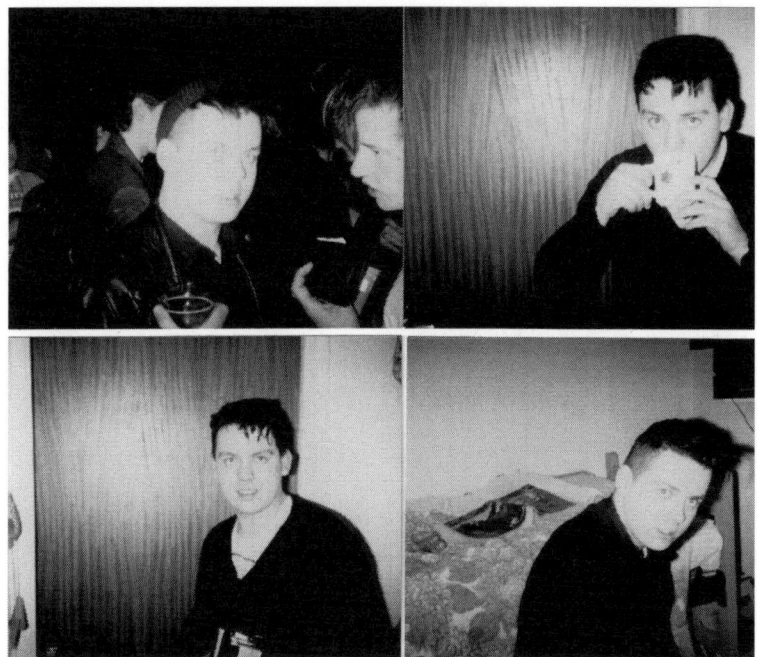

ONE OF THE JOYS OF WORKING FULL-TIME as a teenager was buying records and seeing bands play live. I rented a small room in a large house with many others in Westcliff-on-Sea, Essex. It was known as a student area, where people experiencing poverty and immigrants resided. It was also a place for drugs and sex workers. It was quite seedy back then and, if memory serves me well, it had two sex shops. It was a cheap place to live, so I thought it was fine. I've been used to living in cheap accommodation – our family's rented flat that fell apart years ago, and the council house on the rough estate. Getting a room in a shared house while working full-time was exciting. I was sixteen and constantly meeting new friends.

The shop I worked in was called Paul's Discount Clothing. I began working there at weekends and evenings in 1975, and in 1979 worked full-time on and off, working part-time from 1984–6. There was enough money for rent, food, records, and to go out and see a band play live, so I was happy. I used to love serving people and having conversations about customers' lives.

The kids used to get a buzz from seeing my various coloured hairdos and trying to guess what colour my hair would be the next time they visited. Although I used to argue with him about voting Tory, Paul was a decent boss.

On a Saturday evening on the way home, Paul, my boss and I often visited the record shop along Southchurch Road, The Golden Disc. It was on the way home for both of us. Paul would wait around listening to Michael Jackson (his favourite) in his car, or popped in with me, curious about the strange bands whose records I was searching for and buying. You get a great feeling after searching for an obscure record or coming across something new and unusual. Today, I still feel the same excitement when listening to bands and musicians, such as the Idles, Sleaford Mods, Joanna Newsom, Cate le Bon, Billy Nomates, Squid, Albertine Sarges, Bob Vylan, Katy J Pearson, Yard Act, Dry Cleaning, The Young Fathers, Lisa O'Neill, Baxter Dury, Stick in the Wheel, Gustaff, Aldous Harding, and the list goes on. My passion for music has always been as strong as my passion for art and social justice.

Even though I appreciated punk and electronic music, which dominated the charts in the late 1970s and 1980s, my desire for more raw music from the underground was powerful and needed fulfilment beyond music in the commercial, top-down sphere. I regularly listened to John Peel on Radio 1 late at night on my earphones. One of the many memorable moments was when I heard Ultravox with John Foxx for the first time. It was truly mesmerising. The track was called "Artificial Life", and the lyrics pierced my mind in such a way that I still play the track to this day. The words directly connected to me and reflected my feelings of being trapped in repetitive scenarios and unsure how to change everything. It was profound enough to speak to me at a deep level.

I should have left here years ago
But my imagination won't tell me how
This whirlpool's got such seductive furniture
It's so pleasant getting drowned
So we drink and sink and talk and stalk
With interchangeable enemies and friends
Trying on each other's skins
While we're dying to be born again.

Another essential moment was buying the latest Cabaret Voltaire single, "Silent Command" in 1979. Kelly's Records was a decent record store on the ground floor in the Victoria Shopping Centre, Southend-on-Sea. At that time, my taste in music was becoming even more esoteric and experimental. On that particular day, I visited Kelly's during my lunch break just a few hundred yards away.

In those days shops such as the one I worked in played Radio 1 non-stop, which was great when a track you liked came on, but much of the time, there was an awful lot of rubbish being played, and it sometimes felt like psychological torture, especially when tunes were repeated all the time. Paul loved it, and I suppose I've always been a bit of a music snob, and listening to experimental and challenging music has always had an essence of enjoying the grassroots, political and creative energy for me; it was also art. Cabaret Voltaire's qualities did not disappoint in this regard.

The Cabs were lumped in as part of a punky electro-noise movement referred to as industrial music or industrial beats. In the mid-1970s, these unconventional bands emerged, fusing avant-garde electronic music with the rebellious spirit and style of punk rock. Judging from the various comments by those involved, it wasn't perceived as an actual movement but more of a grassroots cultural shift of DIY noise finding its place in the world. I had already heard Silent Command on John Peel's radio show on BBC 1 late one night.

Kelly's was an interesting record shop selling the latest commercial sounds as well as lesser-known artists. Most of the music placed onto their turntable for customer listening was the most highly publicised merchandise. Still, there were those special moments when a customer came along and asked for something different from the usual blandness. It was my turn to be one of those. I was not consciously trying to upset people and their shopping experience, but perhaps a naughty, playful, punky edge was trying to climb to the surface. The shop assistant put the record on, and the out-of-tune piano faded in. An electronic beat, a German voice began talking, and suddenly started to scream, and the music started. It was truly riveting. Listening to its scratchy and glitchy energy in a shop environment and watching other customers express their distaste and concern was a pleasure. It felt like a small disruption against everyday conformity.

Punk Hangouts and Havens in Essex

I HAVE BEEN USING AN excellent online resource over the last few years that connects me to those I used to hang out with, and frequent gigs and clubs. A website called Southend Punk Rock History 1976-1986, dedicated to saving the history of a significant era and celebrating "the rich diversity of music and creativity that the area spewed forth to an unsuspecting world." Revisiting the site has been invaluable in reminding me how amazing this time was and how many different people I knew back then who were doing amazing things as part of a rich, dynamic, grassroots way of life. Southend had its alternative press in the form of fanzines like *Strange Stories* and *New Crimes*, its punk-friendly shops like Nasty's and Projection Records, and a wealth of venues for bands to play at.

Southend's Focus Youth House was a venue popular with punk bands. It was a progressive community centre run by the local council. It hosted experimental theatre groups that put on plays and drama workshops. Upstairs was the Pine Bar, where many of us met before events and gigs. Focus was an amazing place. From 1979 to the late 1980s, it was a vital grassroots space for up-and-coming bands to play, and there was always a decent audience, with enough fans and visitors to jump around and enjoy the music and support the bands. The youth house was a major part of Southend's alternative music history.

Southend is synonymous with the 1960's mods and rockers, but the town also witnessed another historic movement – punk, whose fashion, music, and philosophy shaped an entire generation.[11]

The bands that played at Focus include The Sinyx, The Icons, The School Bullies, Bleeding Pyles, Death Obsession, The Kronstadt Uprising, The Burning Idols, The Shakers, Empire Backfire, The Prey, The Armless Teddies, Allegiance To No One, The Three Mothers, Stax Century, The Sickies, The Shocks, Autumn Poison, The Beers-In Brothers, Helana Hex, Year Zero & Panic Stricken. Also, The Cards, The Stripey Zebras, Dark

---

[11] 30 years of punk rock. 9th March 2007. *Echo-News.* https://www.echo-news.co.uk/news/1249707.30-years-of-punk-rock/

Deeds on a Lonely Bridge (86-Mix), The Get, Cats Meat Dogs Meat, and many more.

Around this time, I met my first love. Her name was Natalie, and she was a student at the local college who wore punky clothes. Her hair was yellow-blond and spikey. By chance, we sat at the same table upstairs in the bar. Natalie was with another girl discussing bands, and her friend said she thought Siouxsie and the Banshees were the best. Then, out of nowhere, Natalie asked me what I thought. I said that I liked the Slits, Nina Hagen, and Lene Lovich. The conversation moved on to other groups we wanted to see, and then we went downstairs to watch whoever was playing live that night. When I talk about my first love, I think of the person with whom I shared a deep, three-year relationship when we truly loved each other. I had relationships with other young women and a man; the others were either extremely interesting, confusing, dynamic, painful, or fun. But this one with Natalie was more serious. Having said this, there is also Jane, who I was with after Natalie for a few years, and we both moved from Southend to Bristol together, but that's another story discussed later in the book.

The names of the bands listed above who've played at the Focus are a testament to the wild imagination and humour of the local youth. I know most of these bands from that time. I have also been in a few bands in Southend, and one that played at the Focus Centre was Helana Hex. I was the lead singer, wrote the lyrics, played keyboard and the synth now and then, and programmed the drum machine. The main keyboard player was Paul, who had blue spikey hair. Then we had Raymond, a good bass player who was really into punk but also liked Level 42, which we were not happy about. Soon, we got an excellent drummer, Andy, who studied mathematics at the local college.

On Saturdays, many punks and outcasts usually met at the end of the high street in an area known locally as "the green." When it was lunchtime at Paul's Discount Clothing Store, I would pop by and say hello to some pals. Others would arrive later, mid-afternoon. If I walked back and revisited after work, around 6 p.m., those still left, the die-hard punks drinking cheap cider, would be splayed out on their backs, pissed out of their heads. It wasn't a pretty sight. However, they were harmless, and it felt like they were a local feature hanging around at the end of the high street. These days, they'd probably be removed by security or police.

Another haunt was The Grand Hotel in Leigh on Sea, where our group, Helana Hex, played a couple of times. There was also The Blue Boar pub, where we also played. There used to be a music studio around the back of the pub, where I practised and recorded live sessions with various bands. The Grand Hotel was legendary and had bands playing there from 1976. The bands I knew who played there were Stax Century, The Get, The Prey, Kronstadt Uprising, and more. Others were My Life Story and our band Helana Hex. Before she formed Yazoo with Vince Clarke, Alison Moyet's band played their debut there in 1978 in her all-female band, the Vandals, who were based in Basildon. Nix Lowrey of The Quietus interviewed Alison Moyet in 2011. Among other things, she discussed her early times in the punk band The Vandals. Moyet said,

> For me, it really took off with punk, and I think it was less about music than the culture of it – finding yourself amongst a group of freaks you felt more akin to. It was more about the lyricism and the aggression, and entertaining yourself, really. We lived in a new town where we had no money and there was no culture going on so it was a way of us entertaining one another. We would play in car parks or in fields and everyone was in a band whether you could play an instrument or not. That was the joy of punk, really.[12]

Then there's the Crocs – Pink Toothbrush 1980–1985 nightclub, a group on Facebook for anyone who used to go there. Members share photos from that time, memories, music, and general banter. The club was based in Rayleigh, a market town between Chelmsford and Southend-on-Sea, Essex. Before it was renamed Pink Toothbrush, it was called Crocs. Before it changed, Crocs resembled a post-apocalyptic landscape, or a dark street in Berlin, with graffiti everywhere. It was famous for the two live crocodiles in an aquarium inside, which I was always uncomfortable with. Eventually, the club owners gave the reptiles to a zoo, where they learned for the first time that the so-called Crocs were, in fact, alligators. Once the venue became known as Pink Toothbrush, it featured palm trees and resembled a pastiche of a trendy Caribbean nightclub that Wham would have played

---

12 Alison Moyet Interviewed: Only You – The Story & End Of Yazoo. Nix Lowrey. *The Quietus*. May 4th, 2011. https://thequietus.com/articles/06189-alison-moyet-interview-yazoo?

in. Still, during the early 1980s, it was a great venue for brilliant bands such as Fad Gadget, Naked Lunch, Soft Cell, Culture Club, Sex Gang Children, Virgin Prunes, Death Cult, Flesh for Lulu, Clint Eastwood and General Saint, Danse Society, The Damned, Killing Joke, Department S, Siouxsie and the Banshees, Cabaret Voltaire, and many more. Depeche Mode, Alison Moyet, and Culture Club members would attend and dance to music and watch bands play in the early days, with other now-famous names like comedian Phil Jupitus and actor Scroobius Pip.

Gary Tuner, one of the DJs at Crocs, also owned a small clothing shop called Pinups, named after the Bowie album. The clothes were usually made to order. Whenever I had extra cash, I would buy some outrageous outfits and then wear them at Crocs alongside heavy make-up – many of us did. I was unsure whether I was a futurist, a punk, or a new romantic, but mostly punk and post-punk, as I recall now. However, many of us were shifting our identities around in different ways, including exploring our sexuality to find out where we belonged. Many of my friends went further than I would regarding exploring sexual freedoms and/or sexual hedonism. For me personally, even though there were times I experimented, overall, sexuality was an area which felt too confusing to unpack. I have always had a wild side, but it has tended to manifest as social, political, and artistic energy.

Another place in Southend was the Cliff pub in the late 1970s and early 1980s. It was a venue where gays and punks hung out. There were two large downstairs rooms where punks would go and one where the gays usually went. Sometimes, they would cross over into each other's bars. There was another bar upstairs where bands would play and events took place. It was a place where outsiders were accepted and congregated. However, the pub sometimes banned all punks if something like a fight occurred. Some gay non-punk clientele preferred that the pub was not as open to punks and similar unwashed vagabonds. To be honest, they had a point. But, overall, it was a friendly atmosphere. I revisited the pub recently, and even on a Friday night, it lacked the dynamic and edginess it used to have. I think this is because when my peers and I used to go there, it had a grassroots energy, where a feeling of mutual acceptance of being against the establishment was openly appreciated and shared as part of a movement or at least as part of a societal and cultural identity.

The issue of places being less radical or edgy than they used to be does not bother me. It's okay. I believe the spirit of grassroots creativity comes and goes and pops up in different environments, at different times, and anywhere in the world.

Natalie

SOME PEOPLE REMAIN in your mind even though you have not seen them for many years. Natalie is one of those individuals. Through her, I came to understand myself socially, politically, and intellectually in ways I never had before. In truth, we both taught each other an awful lot while we were together as a couple. Natalie was one of the most passionate individuals I had ever known. We began going out in the early 1980s. We were both about 19 and were together for about three and a half years. During this short period, so much changed between us. The world was sculpting us while we actively considered who we wanted to be. Natalie was dedicated to animal welfare, a vegetarian, sometimes vegan, a feminist, and politically inclined towards anarchist ideas like myself. I became a vegetarian, and we explored politics, ideas, and life together. We shared a hunger for social change and knowledge.

When Natalie and Ken first met, it was a memorable experience. Mum, twin sisters, brother, and I were chatting in the front room when Ken entered and said something bigoted. It wasn't unusual, but I can't recall exactly what he said. He was taken aback when Natalie called him out on it straight away. He responded with another cold, hateful insult everyone was supposed to take. Still, Natalie shouted at him, calling him a sexist fucking pig! He then looked at me with his cold, stern eyes, which communicated that he'd hit you if you carried on, and said, Marc, your girl's got a mouth on her. I was at a loss how to respond to either of them. But Natalie helped and said, yes, I've got a mouth, and what will you do about it, hit me? We'd never seen anyone talk to Ken like this and get away with it. However, for some reason, he found it refreshing and, as he left the room, said to me: "You've got a good one there." I found it all excruciating; thankfully, they got on better whenever they met each other in the future.

Natalie's dad, John, was an accountant who spent many years cycling in races across Europe. When I knew him, he had retired from racing and had gained some weight. He had a great sense of humour and loved listening to and watching Tony Hancock. Even though I had heard of this English comedian and actor, it was through John that I got more into his material. My two favourite episodes of his TV shows are "The Blood Donor" and "The Radio Ham." John had a similar stature to Hancock and had quite identical behaviour in some ways, except Hancock's attitude was like a romantic chancer. John, a committed socialist, was deeply supportive of both Natalie and her younger sister, Geraldine.

Natalie's mother, Josephine, was also a socialist and a maths teacher at a local school in Rayleigh, Essex. They were an educated middle-class family. They owned their own home, which was a new build. Josephine said, "Why aren't you famous yet, Marc? Your work is amazing?" I'm not sure when this was said, and I think it may have been during my A levels before I applied for an art foundation course at the same college. I knew my art was good, but didn't know how it fitted into the larger world. My art was raw, political, surreal, and wild in spirit. Also, I knew as much about administration, business, applying for arts funding and networking, as I did about what it was like to be privileged at Eton. A professional art career seemed miles away.

Natalie and I used to regularly visit Crocs nightclub in Rayleigh, Essex, where we danced to alternative punk and electro music, watched great live bands, and dressed up wildly. We'd do the same when seeing bands play in London or elsewhere further out. The bands we saw included New Order, Siouxsie and the Banshees, John Cooper Clarke, The Cramps, The Cocteau Twins, Sisters of Mercy, The Cure, and many more. Sharing urgent, original, free-spirited music with a loved one is a special feeling. I can't imagine being with anyone who wasn't interested in alternative music, like myself. It's such a part of who I am. Natalie and I usually saw bands with friends. Besides Simon Fisher, Steve was also a close friend with whom we'd go and see many gigs.

Natalie and I used to go to protest marches together, mainly in London. In one of the marches, we were chased by a policeman. I'm not sure why, but I can imagine Natalie must have said a few words to him. It was quite an exhilarating experience. We ran at a pace together into different alleyways and across different roads, finding toilets to hide in. We kissed passionately in each other's arms. It all felt very romantic.

Natalie and my Mum were wholeheartedly against misogynist, nasty men. Many a time, they would get together and discuss how useless, idiotic, and violent men are. I didn't disagree. To my Mum and Natalie, I was an honorary woman. Not that I had any wish to be one, but they both discussed the matter and decided that I was a close ally. Politics would also get discussed a lot. We also used to get involved in local activism, such as animal rights and ecology.

I was also studying at Southend College when Natalie was there. Compared to my three A levels, she was doing about eight. She was Learning A-level maths and various languages. I had never met anyone as serious about learning and studying as her. I was dedicated, but Natalie took it all to the next level. It was obvious that she had big ambitions for her future.

Simon and Perry

SIMON AND PERRY WERE PUNKS and close friends in 1981. We used to go and see bands play in London, visit local haunts such as Crocs and the Cliff Pub, and attend various parties. I remember when I first visited Simon's home. One night on our way to Crocs, Simon invited me to stop by his home. As I pushed the gate open, I noticed the curtains twitching and a concerned grey-haired face staring at me as I walked towards the front door. Of course, even before I reached the door, it was obvious that I was considered a troublemaker. And, I suppose I was. However, I felt proud of my outlandish bright red, spikey hair, silver trousers and red plastic mackintosh. I rang the doorbell, and the door opened slowly. His parents were in their sixties, and later that night, I found out Simon was adopted. He was originally born in Liverpool and recently moved to Southend with them.

Typically, I was a mixture of innocent and extremely experimental regarding the clothes I wore. Once, we went to Crocs and on the way stopped off at Simon's girlfriend's house to pick her up. Her parents were typically middle-class; both were commuters for businesses in London, and the only punk or odd outsider they'd ever get close to was their daughter Harriet. When Simon and I walked into their home, her mother immediately laughed at me and ran down to the end of the garden because she couldn't help herself. Admittedly, I did look unusual. I was wearing brown leather jodhpurs, makeup, and other strange things. To me, it felt exciting, but to her mother, it was ridiculous. I think I wanted to run after her and punch her. Instead, because I have always been respectful to my parents, I took the metaphorical punch on the chin and was happy to leave quickly. Once in the club, it felt as if I was with my tribe, and there were many in there, friends and strangers, but all cultural comrades, who looked even wilder than me that evening. I felt at home.

Simon and Harriet were a good punk couple, both glamorous and good-looking. They dated for about three years. After that, Simon spent a long while with many different young women. Some for a short time and others now and then. Each of them was an excellent individual, but Simon had deep emotional problems. He was going through difficult issues that stemmed from him not knowing who his blood parents were, and he was never content and always felt lost. Simon was a warm-hearted and affectionate friend who was very open about these concerns. He was a broken man, searching for something missing within himself. This running theme started quite positively in the form of close friendships and being connected to a grassroots punk tribe.

We were both working full-time – me in the shop and him at the "Access House" credit card offices near Priory Park, in Southend. Years later, the site was closed down and demolished. Perry, Simon's good friend, also worked there. They both didn't like working at the credit card office, but I remember the pay was OK – more than what I was earning anyway. They could afford to buy motorbikes and cars, while I couldn't. This didn't bother me; I couldn't drive. I used to cycle and walk everywhere. Perry was a charming, likeable, black punk. I got to know Perry very well, and we'd all spend our weekends going to clubs and seeing bands play live in London. Sadly, he got stomach cancer. He was almost unrecognisable when I visited him at Southend Hospital. He'd lost over five stone and looked disturbingly pale.

The night before he died, we met in a dream. Perry sat comfortably in a red leather armchair and said he would like to give me a present to remember him by. He slowly pushed himself up from the chair, looking like he did before he caught cancer, and handed me his studded belt. I took the belt and felt honoured to receive such a personal gift. I said thank you, and then he walked away. I woke up that morning believing I had his belt in my room. However, the realisation that it was a dream and that something horrible had happened hit me soon afterwards.

The night before, I stayed at my Mum's. I had to prepare for work, and Mum had already taken the twins, Zoe and Sammy, to school. On the way, a rumbling energy resonated in my body like a physical hum. My eyes were misty and blurred, almost crying. At the time, I still wasn't aware that he was gone. I walked past the school, and Mum was on her way back. She had received a phone call earlier from Perry's parents that he had passed away in the night. As soon as she told me, I felt a thick heaviness engulf my mind, clogging it up like a thick fog. On the way to work, everything around me seemed distant, a long way away. Throughout the day, the distant numbness persisted. It was like a dream, an unhappy one. This heavy, immersive energy stayed with me for weeks. It was difficult to shake off.

The number of punks paying their respects at the funeral was quite a sight. It was well attended and beautiful. Spikey, coloured hair was everywhere, and all who attended tried to look the part. It was a sombre occasion, but also heart-warming to know that so many friends loved him. At the end of the funeral, Perry's mother handed me his studded belt. It felt strange, especially that we had not discussed it before, and because I had dreamt it, and did not in any way expect it to happen in real life. It was a classic three-row pyramid studded leather belt. Following the funeral, I wore it for a while. Because I moved around so many times in my life, I was bound to lose it, and I did, alongside all those other items I wish I still had, such as personal photographs and valuable records I wish I hadn't sold.

Simon changed dramatically after Perry's death. He distanced himself from his punk pals and joined another tribe. Many lived in Canvey, and some of them were rockabilly. They were like us, working class and part of the army reserve forces. This lot was an aggressive bunch and extremely racist, which was weird really because Simon had many friends that were people of colour. It was just a phase though. Following this odd period of hanging out with nasty racists, he split up from that gang, moved, and became a hairdresser.

York Road Market Jobs

YORK ROAD MARKET consisted of small indoor shops. It was originally set up for soldiers needing work after WWI. The shops were mostly run by working-class people and cheap to rent. It was closed between 1999 and 2001. Around 2007, customer numbers picked up. It was like a little Camden with gothic clothing, a bookshop, Gumbi Records, and more.

I used to work there in the early 1980s. Many students from the main college used to work and buy there, and it became quite popular. However, the council was not interested in supporting grassroots sellers, and despite locals asking for investment in the market, it was all demolished and replaced by a car park.[13] It was an area where so much history happened for many Southenders.

Simon used to have a barber shop opposite a café where I used to work when I was 12. My main memory of working there was that I used to cycle three and a half miles and turn up at 6 a.m. It was hard work; I would make fried breakfasts, coffees, and teas, clear tables, and serve all day. Early morning customers were mainly local shopkeepers and builders, who ate breakfast before work. The rugged shopping area boasted quite a strong community.

Over the years, I would leave and then return to work in the market and stalls around the back at weekends. I worked regularly at Gumbi Records in the market between 1985–6. Besides rare records, there was a lucrative demand for live bootleg tape recordings. I had many myself, and one of my tasks working there was to run off copies of bootleg tapes ready for customers.

Recording music on a tape machine and selling, swapping, and buying copies was a subculture. It was all fueled by grassroots energy and the passion of music fan. Record companies said such bootlegging activity negatively impacted sales of commercial releases. However, this dubious

---

13 Southend shoppers remember former York Road market. *Echo news*. 5th April 2023. https://www.echo-news.co.uk/news/23435154.southend-shoppers-remember-former-york-road-market/

assumption was about distancing the subculture from connecting to the music and its societal and cultural contexts. Those who bought these lo-fi mementoes were the "kind of fans who bought an album twice if it came with two different cover designs."[14] Most bootleg cassette tape designs were DIY creations, typed at home on a typewriter and then scanned and printed at the local library.

    I was working out back on the outdoor stalls one day, and my old best friend Bobby's foster mum saw me. She was with his brother Danny. I haven't seen them since we moved to the council estate, but I am unsure why. She was unhappy to see me there and was clear on the matter. Rose expressed disgust towards my scruffy pink hair and said I disappointed her and their family. I was not aware of how snotty she was until then. I didn't know how to respond to her insults and just asked her to leave me alone, and she went off in a huff with Danny, who kept quiet. It hurt me because I used to love them dearly. Rose was unaware that I was at college at the time, working various jobs to survive.

---

14 Bob Leggitt. Myth & Reality: "Home Taping Is Killing Music". *Planet Botch*. 2017. https://planetbotch.blogspot.com/2017/09/myth-reality-home-taping-is-killing.html

Early 1980s Anarchism in Southend

IF YOU'RE GOING TO WRITE about Southend and anarchism, which I am, Graham Burnett is the main guy to talk about. I have heard and seen most of Graham's rhetoric, ideas, and comments over the years, and judging by these, I see that he is not just an anarchist. He's also a green permaculturalist and has been for years. This is his anarchism, and it's diverse. It comes from a place of DIY and grassroots eco-social change. All his endeavours have been on the ground, involved with and organising positive events and projects, changing things for the better. He went to the same school as me, Cecil Jones High, and was a year above me. However, we didn't become friends until we left the school in the early 1980s. We were involved in local punk bands, clubs, punk zines, and activist events. He was in many bands, and the first one I saw him play live with was an anarcho-punk group called Autumn Poison (originally Enola Death). I remember seeing him and core members Sheena Fulton and Paul Brown in 1980 at Focus.

Anarchist fanzines provided a direct outlet for local anarchists to support grassroots culture, offer forums for discussion, and share news about ongoing events. I edited, illustrated and published a few, but Graham was more prolific and also used to publish booklets about anarchism, activism and veganism. I have a strong memory of meeting Graham on the street near the Civic Centre, where he used to work as an administrator for the council, clutching carrier bags full of pamphlets, leaflets, and booklets. He regularly used the council's photocopying machines, staples, and printers. Below is an image from a video about a book he recently published on Southend Zines featuring New Crimes, of which he published seven editions, ending in 1984.

We used to meet outside McDonald's and Burger King in the high street and protest outside their shops, against their use of "using lethal poisons to destroy vast areas of Central American rainforest to create grazing pastures for cattle to be sent back to the States as burgers and pet food."[15] Burnett often joined other vegans and activists on early morning hunt saboteur missions. I went on one with Natalie, which became a scuffle between an ALF (Animal Liberation Front) member and one of the huntsmen. It was quite a culture shock coming across, for the first time, rich men on horses with whips, trying to kill foxes. For me, it was very much a class thing, and for Natalie, who was vegan (I was vegetarian), it was more about saving animals. Disrupting rich people and their blood sports activities while visiting the countryside was exciting. The difference in wealth was clear: we were in direct conflict with the landed gentry and Tory councillors, who viewed people such as myself as low life.

15 Starvation in the Third World and destruction of rainforest. McSpotlight, June 1997. https://www.mcspotlight.org/case/trial/verdict/verdict_jud1d.html

After Autumn Poison disbanded, Graham and Paul occasionally collaborated under the title 'Love Over Law' and released several cassette albums in the late 1980s and early 1990s. Graham had also run the 'Pritty Toons Press' for several years, producing local fanzines such as his own, New Crimes, and Necrology and Confidential Waste. Nowadays, he runs permaculture workshops and various eco-friendly schemes.[16]

Occasionally, Graham raided animal testing laboratories with his green anarchist crew. I joined one such raid myself but was asked to stay in a van and not get involved because I'd get in the way. It was all very quick and dark, about four in the morning. Most of those taking part were ALF members, and the liberated animals ranged from beagles to guinea pigs, rabbits, and rats. After one of these raids, Natalie and I popped around Burnett's small house in the Prittlewell area for dinner and wine. His front room was immediately accessible from the street, and the place always looked like a squat. It was a sight to see all the Crass posters, similar paraphernalia on the walls, and many of his DIY zines. When we entered, the

---

16   Steven Pegrum. Southend Punk Rock History 1976- 1986. https://www.southendpunk.com/html/autumnwp.html

television was on and he was watching Eastenders with three white ex-lab rats. All four of them looked very content with each other.

More recently, our art group Furtherfield, based in Finsbury Park, London, collaborated with Burnett's organisation, Spiralseed, to run permaculture workshops in our Commons lab. Furtherfield hosted Spiralseed's Design 4 ACTION! Permaculture Courses in Finsbury Park 2015–18.[17]

Burnett has published many books about permaculture and veganism and in 2022, a book titled *Southend on Zine*. It comprises 200 pages celebrating 50 years of voices and stories from Southend's alternative press and fanzine underground. "The book is both a history and a celebration of Southend's often forgotten 'alternative' and DIY culture, as told through the pages of the fanzines, people's papers, and community magazines made in the town between 1971 and 2021."[18] Reading the book reminded me of many past friends and associates. Too often, voices and stories on the ground are drowned out by top-down-driven commercialism over substance and societal contexts. Burnett's book gives valuable recognition to some truly great individuals and groups who otherwise would have been forgotten. In a way, these people, including Graham and many others featured in this book, have built something special, usually out of nothing and through struggle from the ground up. These people share a drive to organise life and culture for themselves and each other and not just accept what is given/imposed. Without people like Graham and others working to make a difference from a grassroots level, life would be unbearable for those suffering under austerity policies, which drive people into deeper poverty and harm their mental and physical health.

17 Spring Into Action: Permaculture Design Course at Furtherfield Commons. Furtherfield. 01/09/2015 – 29/02/2016. https://www.furtherfield.org/spring-into-action-permaculture-design-course-at-furtherfield-commons/
18 'Southend On Zine' Book – *Fifty Years of voices and stories from Southend's alternative press and fanzine underground* – by Graham Burnett – Kickstarter. https://southendpunk.com/html/sozinegb.html

Cha, Cha, Cha, Changes

SINCE I WAS A TEENAGER, I have been haunted by David Bowie's song, "Changes." The lyrics spoke to me deeply, reflecting what I was going through in my life. I'm sure it wasn't unusual, and many others out there have felt the same. It was released as a single from the album Hunky Dory in January 1972. An amazing album. It was one of those records Natalie and I would mellow out to, like The Smiths in the 1980s, connected to a dysfunctional and outsider youth. Bowie echoed his sentiments more than a decade before Morrissey, when changes happening to us were constant.

As we grow up, we undergo constant transformation and changes in our brains and bodies.

Looking back at the three years of my relationship with Natalie, it feels like another life.

The cliché that time speeds up as you get older is true. Time is like an unstoppable juggernaut, and no one can control it. Those three years were jam-packed with incredible learning, fun, emotional tensions, and deep love. Being with Natalie was intense, not only because we were both dedicated to bettering ourselves as human beings, but also because we were both caught in a flux of changes. We noticed some of these changes in ourselves and each other, but other changes were more fundamental. Stuff that you can't see when you're in the middle of it all. These changes are bigger, and even though we know of them, they can mutate in ways we can't see and spring surprises on us if we're not looking.

One of the things that has always caught me off guard is the very thing that has defined my life from birth to now. In retrospect, I'm always surprised by how blind I am to what turns out to be an insidious flaw in my character. This flaw is that I tend to forget that others view me as lower class, which you can forget once you've put aside your differences. Still, the systems we live in remind us who we are and who we are predetermined to be by default. This default lurks in the background, is insidious, and can cause immense trauma. The experiences of certain incidents leave scars that stick like glue to one's delicate soul – so much so that it takes decades to heal. My breakup with Natalie left one of those big scars.

Yet, it should have been so obvious that you could kick yourself asking "Why didn't I realise what would happen"?

It wasn't just the deep gap she left inside me. It was also a reminder that she was middle-class and that the world was designed to support her in a different way. Of course, we were both aware of each other's class backgrounds and enjoyed learning from each other about our differences. Yet, our future never came up while we were together. Things came to a head when it was her time to leave college. Unbeknownst to me, Natalie had already been accepted for a degree in Brussels. The degree was a European studies course to prepare her for work as a translator for the European Union. Before she told me about it, there were signs that our future was unstable. It was like an invisible force was pulling our strings from above, influencing our actions and emotions towards each other.

Natalie had rarely insulted me before, but it became a regular occurrence towards the end. Things were getting intense. One time, when we were sat at my mum's dining table, she got carried away and had gone too far. She was cruel and offensive regarding my aspirations and shouted that I was a waste of time and would never amount to anything. I wasn't sure what was happening, but her putting me down made me feel useless and embarrassed. I couldn't hold back any longer, and I stuffed a sandwich in her mouth to shut her up. As soon as I had done the spontaneous bad deed, a silence shrouded the room and my Mum and I watched Natalie tear up. I immediately regretted what I'd done. However, seeing her crying instead of shouting at me was a relief.

It's confusing when a loved one suddenly treats you differently, and you feel like an obstacle to their path in life. It is demeaning, confusing, and a desperately lonely experience. The other time things got too much was when we were at a Jesus and Mary Chain gig in London. They had just released their first album, *Psychocandy*, in 1985. It was a very noisy, ear-thumping, and enjoyable performance. A good friend, Stuart, a record company A&R man, knew some band members and invited us to the after party. We all ended up in someone's flat nearby. Natalie felt quite distant that evening, and I wasn't sure why. We lost each other, and I couldn't find her. I decided to leave and caught the early morning train back to Southend around 4 a.m.

I hadn't heard from her for the rest of the weekend. On Monday, I worked one of my part-time days at Paul's Discount Clothing store. Natalie surprised me with a visit at lunchtime. On another road behind the row of shops was a small, shabby park, Warrior's Square. As we walked there, I knew something was up. She was cagey and quivering slightly. We sat down on a bench, and it all felt weird. Natalie informed me that she had a sexual encounter with the bass player at the after party, which was why I couldn't find her. I wasn't sure whether to believe her, but it seemed true enough. Then she told me she was leaving me and was off to Brussels soon. So, there it was, a double whammy. Natalie had slept with someone else and was leaving me for Europe. I felt so small and worthless, knowing that she was going to have an amazing new life while I would be left behind like a small-town idiot with no hope.

About a year later, I visited her with Steve, my best friend at the time. Natalie was renting a flat in Anderlecht, Brussels. We approached the building where she was staying and were just about to enter when a load of clothes cascaded above us, hitting the pavement. Natalie was leaning out of a window on the fourth floor, shouting at a guy who had just left the building. Steve and I walked up the stairs and knocked on the door; she answered with a smile. It was as if the love was still there between us. We all got on well and discussed what we were all up to. That evening, we all went to see The Cure play live, which was an amazing gig. Their set was long, about two and a half hours, perhaps more. However, no one wanted it to end.

That night, I slept in the same bed as Natalie. It was lovely to be holding her in my arms again. We tried to have sex, but it didn't feel right, and to be honest, we were both not that interested. Instead, we cuddled each other through the night. At that time, I was with another woman, Jane, and we had discussed with each other what may occur when I visit Natalie. Jane was very relaxed about it all. I suppose visiting Natalie provided the closure I needed to move on.

For years, Natalie and my Mum continued meeting each other. They still got along very well, but Mum never told me what they talked about, and I never knew when their meetings took place. At first, it felt strange, but I forgot about it as time passed until Natalie's name was mentioned. In the early 1990s, Natalie invited my Mum to her wedding. Mum said Natalie didn't want me to come because she still loved me. I wasn't sure if Mum was trying to make me feel better. What surprised me was hearing that

Natalie was going to lose her last name. That wasn't the woman I knew. However, I was in the dark in respect of the circumstances.

After that last meeting in Belgium, we never saw each other again. Many times, I wondered what her life was like now. Does she have kids and live abroad or in the UK? Like with other old acquaintances, I have looked for her online. She seems to be off the grid, but it's just her last name that is different. I know Natalie would feel very sad about Mum dying. At the funeral, on 15 Oct 2020, I half expected Natalie to show up and give her condolences. But no. It's a funny thing. The death of Mum was poignant in so many ways. I realised that I was not only grieving her death, but also my relationship with Natalie that ended all those years back.

Sympathy for the Runt

WHEN I WAS 22, I lived with Rick Buckley, a filmmaker and artist friend. We shared a first-floor flat near London Road, Westcliff, in Southend. We were students at Southend College of Art and Design. He worked part-time at the local postal sorting office, and I still worked part-time at Paul's Discount Clothing Store. I also took on other jobs for extra money, some quite depressing and demeaning, discussed elsewhere in this book.

As usual, contemporary music was the feral spirit mirroring and criticising the backdrop of England's social issues of the time. Many sonic anthems act like beacons, reminding us of past experiences, cultural dialogues, and societal contexts. Rick and I loved Derek Jarman's short film incorporating three music videos for The Smiths: Panic, There Is a Light That Never Goes Out, and The Queen Is Dead. The latter was never released as a single, but may as well have been: it was regularly played on the radio and in clubs. All three songs are poignant and represent disquiet about the wrath of Thatcher's Britain. Earlier, Jarman directed *Jubilee* (shot 1977, released 1978), in which "Queen Elizabeth I of England was transported [...] to a desolate and brutal wasteland ruled by her twentieth-century namesake." In 1987, Jarman's following film *The Last of England* explored "memories, thoughts and fantasies, assembled in a collage of styles consisting of a quasi-documentary chronicle, with home movies and video," to vent his fury at Thatcher's England. *Jubilee* presented us with a nihilistic world caught in the throes of punk rebellion, and *The Last of England* offered an apocalyptic vision of the nation's future as a homophobic and repressive totalitarian state.

In order to appreciate any of these films, you didn't need to be a punk, a Smiths fan, or queer. You just had to be living in a way the government didn't value, respect, and ultimately reject. As with most totalitarian governments, they actively attack the misrepresented, exploit their vulnerabilities, and use them as scapegoats to distract the masses from society's actual problems. Society's rejects were being demolished from a great height with all the brutal force a state could get away with. And it did get away with it. In 1985, another enemy of the Tory and tabloid class was viciously dealt with. New Age Travellers were "ambushed with extraordinary violence by around 14,000 police from six counties and the Ministry of Defence in what has become known as the Battle of the Beanfield."[19] It was executed with the predictable coldness of a bad parent or an authoritarian bully. The travelling convoy was trying to settle near Stonehenge for the 12th annual free festival in fields opposite the ancient temple on Salisbury Plain. The police violently clubbed pregnant women with truncheons as they held babies.[20] In contrast to the dreadful onslaught wreaked upon these people, the tabloid press portrayed them "as dangerous, dirty anarchists threatening Britain's heritage at Stonehenge with their festival." One of my friends, Hippy Jo, was part of these convoys. When he returned to Southend, I heard disturbing stories of people being violently attacked and hospitalised. Another punk friend came back bruised and shocked by how the government treated them.

Southend was home to many activists in the mid-1980s. There was, among others, a strong anarchist, vegan movement. The bands they were listening to were Chumbawamba, Crass, and The Poison Girls. It was all very tribal. To be accepted into the green anarchists' fold, you needed to look the part, that is wear green, scruffy army surplus clothes and no leather shoes. Paul's Discount Clothing Store used to sell stuff like that. I wore such clothes now and then but I was more of a shabby goth(-ish) punk and often wore DM boots. I got on with one of them, Graham Burnett. The other green anarchists were snotty towards me, but I wasn't bothered.

Rick's sister, Debbie, stayed with us briefly, borrowing our shared art studio at the back of the flat. I got on with her very well; she was a dedicated vegan. I was a vegetarian and struggling to be a vegan. I enjoyed eggs and cheese too much. However, we did relate to each other regarding animal welfare. One morning, we were cycling down the usually busy London Road. I was going to college, and Debbie to work. On the way, we found a dead cat on the curb. We picked it up, and it had already reached

19 2023 June | Andy Worthington. https://www.andyworthington.co.uk/2023/06/page/2/
20 Worthington, Andy. It's 30 Years Since Margaret Thatcher Trashed the Travellers' Movement at the Battle of the Beanfield. 2015. https://www.andyworthington.co.uk/2015/06/01/its-30-years-since-margaret-thatcher-trashed-the-travellers-movement-at-the-battle-of-the-beanfield/

the stage of *rigor mortis*. It was strange to lift a dead animal up, which resembled a stiff piece of cardboard. We cycled back to the flat and asked the downstairs neighbour, Dave, if it was OK to bury the cat in his back garden. He said yes, so we did.

Debbie soon left the flat to live elsewhere. She wanted to live nearer to work. Ironically, it was a local farm just outside Southend. About a month after she had left, we began to smell a horrible, rotting stink in the back studio where she had stayed. We went to investigate. Rick opened a cupboard, and underneath all kinds of junk, we found a shoe box. Inside was a rotting piglet with maggots eating away at its reeking corpse. It felt as if we had found a dead baby decomposing in a cardboard coffin. The smell was awful, but not an evil one. The complexity of this discovery was hard for Rick and me to articulate. It was an odd, mutual recognition of something unsaid. We shared a weird feeling that this piglet symbolised something – both to Debbie, and to us.

Rick asked her why she'd left a dead piglet in a shoebox in the studio cupboard. She said that the farm was throwing rejected piglets over a fence. This caused her distress, as she was vegan and believed all animals should be given a chance to live. Like me, Debbie opposed how capitalism exploited animals as mass-produced food and in animal testing in cosmetics. It was more than just a diet; it was a radical way of critiquing the relationship between humans, society, and animals, and it stood against mass industrialisation in farming and the commodification of animals as assumed products and fodder. Debbie asked the farmer why he threw runt piglets over the fence to die. He said they were useless and a waste of space, time, and money. Debbie was not happy about the situation at all.

One day on the farm, she heard a squealing noise from behind a fence. She looked over and saw that a piglet was still alive amongst the other dead ones. That day, Debbie left work early, returning to the flat with the piglet. She brought it back in a towel and hid it in her room. We were not allowed in the room at the time and were unaware that the reason was because she had what was possibly a new friend. However, the animal did not live long and died within a few days. Debbie said she was traumatised and hid the dead piglet in the cupboard in a shoebox and that she had genuinely intended to bury it. But in the end, she could not face doing it after leaving for her new home. It was left to Rick and I to dispose of the rotting animal and get the room fumigated.

Initially we reacted with anger, especially Rick. But, because all three of us came from tough working-class backgrounds, and we all – at some level – sympathised with the runt's disposition. We were all the rejected – tossed over the fence and left to face our precarious fates alone.

The Useless Sea

ONE OF THE MANY JOBS I had in Southend-on-Sea while doing my Art Foundation Course at Southend College of Art and Design was making holes in marble bases for trophies. It was part-time, and my boss was also my landlord. The extra work helped to pay the rent. Tony was an ex-bouncer and was keeping himself fit and stocky by lifting weights at home and at the gym. His wife Harriet had a soft spot for me because she knew my stepdad from the late sixties when they were both mods. They had gone out together and travelled to various places, including Brighton, with their crowd of mods on scooters.

When I moved into my rented room in a house owned by Tony and Harriet, she knocked on my door with champagne to celebrate my moving in, which was very generous of her. I invited her in and we popped the cork and sipped the sparkly. Harriet and I talked about Ken and the adventures they once had. They used to enjoy Northern soul music and dance for days, partly fuelled by amphetamines, or "speed."[21] I found it odd that my landlady would be so forthcoming regarding her past relationship with my stepdad, but also very refreshing.

It was good of Tony to offer me some work, although it was very tough. It involved a variety of jobs, including operating a forklift truck to move large crates of marble around at the warehouse. My main responsibility, however, was drilling holes into trophy bases. I also worked part-time at Paul's Discount Clothing Store, selling clothes and army and navy surplus. On top of this, I was studying part-time at the college as a mature student. I've always had a job of some sort, and I've plenty of shit ones. One job I'll mention with a hint of bitterness is when I was part of a small crew travelling in a van selling kitchenware. I'd have to knock on doors and pretend I was unemployed and just out of prison and going straight, in

---

21 Northern soul: making a scene. David Buckingham. https://davidbuckingham.net/growing-up-modern/young-soul-rebels-soul-scenes-in-seventies-britain/northern-soul-making-a-scene/

need of a spot of luck and money. Many people said no, and many told me to fuck off. It was soul-destroying.

We drove along the Southend seafront to Tony's marble warehouse. Somehow, we got onto the subject of the sea itself and said that I was glad the Tory council hadn't built a marina that would damage the environment and wildlife. Tony retorted aggressively, "What use is the sea? It's doing nothing for us out there. It's not making any money." I answered that fishermen relied on the sea for years, and wasn't it great that capitalism wasn't smothering everything with its greedy mitts? He wasn't having any of it and said, "You're not a communist or a socialist, are you?" I said, "Probably, I don't know! I thought I was more of an anarchist."

Masters of the Universe

I HAVE ALWAYS REGRETTED a particular incident. It's one of those silly things that could have been dealt with differently, but one's mind and situation dictated the outcome, not common sense. I was still sharing a flat with Rick, and we were on the Art Foundation Course at the Southend of Art and Design. I had taken a brief break from working at Paul's store because I needed to spend more time on college work and developing my art.

One late Saturday afternoon, I arrived home after a shift at Tony's warehouse, feeling tired after moving loads of marble crates around with a forklift truck. I walked up the stairs, and Rick was in the front room upstairs playing 1960s psychedelic music on his record player with about four of his friends. I stepped into the room to say hello and noticed they were high on mushrooms, loafing around on the floor and the sofa. Rick asked if I wanted any. At first, I said no because I just wanted to relax. However, my bedroom was next door to the front room, and the music was loud. I decided to have some and then retire to the back studio and rest.

I couldn't relax because the mushrooms were too strong. So, I started to make cheese on toast, and as I was in the middle of doing that, the doorbell rang downstairs. Rick ran to the kitchen and said, "I can't answer that!" Since I wasn't as far gone as him and his mates, I proposed to answer the door while they hid in the front room. It turned out it was Paul from the shop. He never visited the flat, so something must have been wrong. He looked the most serious I'd ever seen him, and because I had worked for him since I was a teenager, I was familiar with all his different moods.

He asked if he could come in, and foolishly I agreed. We walked up the stairs to the sounds of psychedelic music coming from the front room's door. We went to the kitchen, and I offered him some cheese on toast, which he declined. He stood just outside the kitchen, leaning on the door frame. I put the food on a plate, and thought that perhaps it wasn't the right time to eat. By this time, the mushroom high was starting to get a bit stronger, and when Paul asked for his Masters of the Universe toys back, I laughed. I'm not sure if he was aware that I was stoned, but the paranoia was kicking in, and I was losing all sense of reality.

I was meant to paint two characters, Skeletor and He-Man, from "He-Man and the Masters of the Universe" a 1980s animated TV series for his son's bedroom wall. I was good at this kind of thing. Years before, I had painted various shop-centred scenarios on walls inside and outside the store so that it would have been a breeze. But life took over, and even though I made a start, I couldn't find the time to finish it.

I left the kitchen briefly to get the figures. When I returned them to Paul, they were wrapped in tin foil; I have no idea why. He said thank you coldly and then walked down the stairs and left the building. Thankfully, we were able to patch the relationship up a few months later. Yet, whenever I remember this moment, I wince, wishing it had never happened. I felt vulnerable since he decided to visit when I was high on mushrooms. Also, he considered me a stable lad, someone who managed to sort their life out. Paul had always been good to me.

The Shame of Leaving and Returning

MY FIRST ATTEMPT TO LEAVE Southend turned out to be a humiliating disaster. In 1986, I was accepted for an art degree at Chelsea College. It took a bit of wrangling to find a cheap place to live in London with my girlfriend, Jane. The whole process was quite traumatic, but it was outweighed by a very exciting feeling that I would be a student at a London University. However, it all went wrong for me once we had moved to London. A couple of weeks into my degree, I was told my grant hadn't come through or didn't exist. It was all very confusing because I had assurance from the art lecturer at Southend Art College that they'd sorted it all out. When I tried to contact him, the admin told me he'd left on sabbatical, and they were unsure how to contact him. I had heard he was in India. I was told to leave the University, so we had no choice but to return to Southend.

Coming back to Southend was embarrassing. I felt like an idiot. I had spent weeks before leaving saying goodbye to many friends and telling them that I was going to start a new life in another part of the country. Some took it as a snub, me leaving them behind. It was impossible to fulfil my desire to become who I wanted to be in Southend. For years, I knew this day had to come, and there's nothing sadder than saying goodbye or trying to leave and never getting to it. Even though I loved my friends dearly and did not want to hurt them, I was dying inside and needed to get out before I did something stupid and killed myself.

During my foundation course, most of my peers came from middle-class backgrounds and had already figured out their finances and life administration. In contrast, I felt like a clueless child, struggling to navigate the path toward a degree while everyone else seemed to manage with ease. It became painfully clear – though I had always suspected – that I had never been taught how to handle the practical aspects of life. In a capitalist world, this skill is essential for survival. I had plenty of talents, but developing the mindset and habits needed for stability requires years of conditioning, often instilled by parents from an early age. I began to feel like a fraud, as if I were pretending to be someone I wasn't. Who was

I to think I could be an artist? The idea seemed laughable – just a foolish boy chasing an impossible dream.

As my peers from the foundation course began their new and amazing adventures at various universities across the UK, Jane and I had to return to Southend. We ended up in a bedsit on York Road. If anyone reading this is aware of York Road, it's the infamous, druggy red-light area of Southend. Although, to be honest, it was fine. Nothing scary happened; it's just that most people living there were poor and living in small, rented flats. My earlier years on the council estate were more troubling. Our bedsit was on the third floor, and many people lived in the building, with the landlord and landlady living at the bottom. It was cheap, and they never hassled anyone. They gave their tenants their privacy. Our bedsit was one large room with a kitchen, which we loved. We even had a bed that fitted into the wall. It felt quite novel.

Jane took another art course at college and found work in the Body Shop, and I took on two part-time jobs. I returned to my old shop, Paul's Discount Clothing Store, and worked two days a week as a technician at Southend Art College. It was heartbreaking to see all the new hopeful students arrive while my year was gone, and I should have gone also. The deep feeling of failure was eating away at me.

A New Life

UNEXPECTEDLY, we received a letter from a couple of friends, Dick and Tina, who asked us if we were interested in relocating to a farm that they had recently moved to in Somerset. Dick and Tina were a couple in their forties who I used to know when I was at college. They were an interesting couple who supported me emotionally, intellectually, and financially. They bought some of my paintings when they lived in Southend. Their passion for contemporary art and thinking was refreshing. And, even though I had other friends who were intelligent and critical about society, culture, and the world, Dick and Tina had something extra. After the Chelsea Art School disaster, their wisdom and knowledge about lesser-known artists and cultural contexts helped me understand that there were alternative routes to becoming an artist. They read interesting books, old and new, and listened to good music; they engaged in politics, and discussed contemporary art, aesthetics, and social issues. What I especially enjoyed about them both was their frankness on various subjects. The fact they came from working-class backgrounds added a nuanced understanding between us.

Their invitation was welcome news. Jane and I were going stir-crazy in Southend, she was getting depressed and we desperately needed a way out. Jane's parents were very religious, especially her father, who always judged people as sinners. Whenever I visited her home in the countryside near Maldon, her dad would be spouting some nonsense about how she's a Jezebel Whore of Satan. He was a deeply bitter, angry man. Her mother only talked about fashion and beauty and was extremely whimsical, always saying that Jane was ugly and wasting her life being an artist and choosing to be with a useless poor man such as me.

After I had helped Jane escape her family home, she had deep concerns about her older brother, whom she felt guilty about leaving behind. He was suffering from clinical depression and schizophrenia. Jane was alarmed when hearing her family had had Jonathon sectioned after the police had contacted her after he had run amok in Maldon's town centre. Jonathon was a tall, strong man in his early thirties, and it had taken eight police officers to apprehend him. He was allowed back to her parents' home after a few months. When her mother informed her of this, Jane was determined to visit them and see him.

Jonathon was on house arrest and couldn't walk outside far beyond the house's perimeter. I hadn't been there since before Jane had escaped her parents' clutches. The home was a lovely country cottage. I always felt strange when horrible people were wealthy and lived in beautiful homes. If there is a God, then it isn't a just one. The dining room was at the front of the house, right near the entrance. It was a large room with a long wooden table that could sit ten people. We all sat down, and Jonathon was there too, all quiet. The food was ready and we all closed our eyes as Jane's father began his prayers. I opened one eye, looked around, and noticed Jane's brother had his eyes open, staring straight ahead. His eyes were glazed, and he wasn't present. His medication must have been very strong.

Still, he must have known what was happening around him, even if his engagement with his family and me was limited. Jane found the whole experience upsetting as her parents belittled him as a constant nuisance and a burden on their lives. Jane's father said, "I don't know where his evil is from, not our family," speaking in front of Jonathon in the third person. As far as he was concerned, everything outside the vicinity of their pretty cottage was evil. Jane found it very difficult to stand up to her parents. There was so much complaining and hatred towards the world between her father and mother that it was hard for her to find her own voice. When we left, Jane was disturbed by her brother being held captive. There wasn't much we could do.

So, when Dick and Tina offered us this life-changing option, we grabbed it. It was a lovely farmhouse, large enough for us all, including Tina's daughter Taryn. The property was rented from a farmer friend they knew.

Our rent was very cheap. Jane and I had to leave our jobs and sign on as unemployed. I had been saving some money for leaving Southend – a couple of thousand.

Dick and I made extra cash by collecting fallen and cut-down trees from local forest rangers at a reasonable price, and we'd saw and chop the wood and sell it on to people in Bristol. Jane and I had a large bedroom on the ground floor and shared the rest of the house. I had never seen an Aga Range Cooker before.

Jane and I enjoyed new daily rituals on the farm. Hers involved staying in bed until 9 a.m. and reading, followed by a day of painting. Mine would be getting up at 8 a.m., stepping outside the cottage, and walking across a field located at the back of the building, which harboured a few cows. About three-quarters of a mile away was the local Congresbury Yeo River. I would sit there for about an hour watching and listening to the sound of a waterfall. The sound and visuals of the water gushing down the rocks were hypnotic. It was all completely new to me. There was the nagging feeling that I didn't deserve this, that it was wrong, and that I was betraying my class. Not only that, but I was also going to wake up and find that it was all a dream. But these anxious and negative concerns soon evaporated, and I got into the flow of this wonderful new life. This heaven was real. I closed my eyes and felt the subtle touch of the wind and air as they brushed against my skin. I was no longer captive to circumstance.

Haywood Editions is a new series of specially printed books from Minor Compositions, offering an alternative to the standard, trade-published editions of our titles. These editions are produced without barcodes and will not circulate through the commercial book trade. Instead, they are sold directly to readers and comrades. Haywood Editions are printed to a higher standard than the conventional trade versions, and in the spirit Big Bill Haywood channeled when he said that "nothing is too good for the working class." We believe that books meant to spark critical thought and collective imagination deserve to be made, and read, with care and attention.

By purchasing Haywood Editions directly from us, you're not only receiving a finer book, but also helping sustain our work. The return from direct sales goes back into covering the costs of producing books and making them freely available online as open access publications, ensuring that these ideas circulate as widely as possible.

Haywood Editions: nothing is too good for the working class — or for its books.